From Bunker Hill to Baghdad

From Bunker Hill to Baghdad

True Stories of America's Veterans

Patrick Mendoza

LIBRARIES UNLIMITED

AN IMPRINT OF ABC-CLIO, LLC
Santa Barbara, California • Denver, Colorado • Oxford, England

Library of Congress Cataloging-in-Publication Data

Mendoza, Patrick M.
  From Bunker Hill to Baghdad : true stories of America's veterans /
Patrick Mendoza.
    pages cm
  Includes bibliographical references and index.
  ISBN 978-1-59884-466-5 (hardcopy : alk. paper) — ISBN 978-1-59884-467-2
(e-book)   1. United States—Armed Forces—Biography   2. Veterans—
United States—Biography.   3. United States—History, Military.   I. Title.
  U52.M47   2014
  355.0092'273—dc23   2013046140

ISBN: 978-1-59884-466-5
EISBN: 978-1-59884-467-2

18   17   16   15   14   1   2   3   4   5

This book is also available on the World Wide Web as an eBook.
Visit www.abc-clio.com for details.

Libraries Unlimited
An Imprint of ABC-CLIO, LLC

ABC-CLIO, LLC
130 Cremona Drive, P.O. Box 1911
Santa Barbara, California 93116-1911

This book is printed on acid-free paper ∞

Manufactured in the United States of America

Contents

Foreword vii
Preface ix
Introduction xi

REVOLUTIONARY WAR

Chapter 1   "The Devil Himself Could Not Catch Him":
Francis Marion 1

WAR OF 1812

Chapter 2   The Voodoo Queen and the Pirate: Marie Leveau
and Jean Lafitte 9

MEXICAN WAR

Chapter 3   For God? Or for Country?: John Riley and the
San Patricios of the Mexican War . . . . . , , ... 17

THE WAR BETWEEN THE STATES

Chapter 4   It All Started in His Front Yard: Wilmer McLean 25

INDIAN WARS

Chapter 5   To Serve Proud and Free: Isaiah Mays 33

SPANISH AMERICAN WAR

Chapter 6   To Walk Softly and Carry a Big Stick: Theodore
Roosevelt 41

WORLD WAR I

Chapter 7   To Vanish in the Morning: Blanche Hennebery
and George MacCrae 45
Chapter 8   We Laid Aside the Citizen: Joe Angelo and the
Veterans' Bonus March 51
Chapter 9   The Fighting Quaker: Smedley Darlington Butler 59
Chapter 10   A Miracle in the Trenches: Robert Hulse 69

WORLD WAR II

Chapter 11   The Last Acoma: Sam Antonio 75
Chapter 12   The First Son and the Second Marines: James
Roosevelt and Carlson's Raiders. 85
Chapter 13   From the Navy Hymn to Davy Jones' Locker:
Gordon Skinner. 93
Chapter 14   In the Shadow of Giants: Ray Bauml 105

KOREAN WAR

Chapter 15   No Greater Love: Bryant Womack 121
Chapter 16   A Nurse's Story: Jonita Ruth Bonham 127

VIETNAM WAR

Chapter 17   The Day "Doc" Goss Became a Nurse: Jim Goss. 135
Chapter 18   Pardo's Push: Bob Pardo. 141
Chapter 19   The Sailor: Michael Peters 149

IRAQ AND AFGHANISTAN

Chapter 20   Immigrant Soldier: Cecelia Vivar 155

Sources 161
Index 169

Foreword

In these pages by the nationally known author and storyteller, Pat Mendoza, we find the very personal perspectives of time and space, service and sacrifice, and lives forever changed by war and conflict. As diverse as the various wars themselves, Pat has been able to articulate, in a very clear manner, the stories of some great Americans. From the famous to the nearly forgotten, these individuals and their stories touch a chord that rings with the clarion call of service to our nation and service to our fellow man.

The common fabric woven through the stories in this well-written book is the concept of an individual's commitment to something greater than self—whether from past decades, found in the skillful tactics, and leadership of Francis Marion in the birth of a new republic; or the gallantry of Corporal Isaiah Mays in the westward expansion of the nation; or the humble countenance of Ray Bauml of the famed Carlson's Raiders of Marine Corps lore; or the ingenuity and quick thinking of Bob Pardo and his incredible aviation feat; or the absolute devotion of Jim Goss, who repeatedly risked his life in answering the call "Corpsman Up" to administer medical care to his wounded comrades-in-arms; or to the current decade and the warriors of Iraq and Afghanistan who continue to serve with distinction in this era of persistent conflict.

Whether they knew it at the time or not, each of the individuals of whom Pat writes embodied the very essence of selfless, sacrificial service to others for a cause greater than themselves.

Yes, this book is also worth the reading to remind us all of the personal nature of war and conflict, and how blessed we are as a nation to have the few who answer the call to defend and serve. And for those warriors who were fortunate to return from war, their service did not end when they hung up their uniforms. They went on to make lasting contributions in their chosen fields and in their communities, and they continue to do so today.

In *From Bunker Hill to Baghdad*, Pat Mendoza has provided an enjoyable pathway through history with stepping stones of individual accounts of inspiration, hope, service, and sacrifice that may not otherwise have been recorded and stories that may have been forever lost to the greater story of the indomitable human spirit of the American Warrior. The book honors that spirit.

Ward Nickisch
Colonel, U.S. Army, Retired

Preface

Yet today I consider myself the luckiest man on the face of the earth.

—Lou Gehrig

I found, in fact, that I was one of the luckiest men on the face of the earth, because of my wife Dona.

Just months before, I had signed a contract with my publisher, Barbara Ittner (Barbara, thank you for keeping my book alive and your support), to write this book. I had already started my manuscript when I was asked to perform in Tennessee, at the Haunting on the Hills Storytelling Festival. Shortly after my arrival, I was greeted with a massive intracranial stroke.

Had I not been in capable and credible hands, I wouldn't be here to tell you my story. Tom and Faye Woodan watched over me during a harrowing ambulance ride through the mountains of Tennessee. A couple days later, I vaguely remember my wife Dona and daughter Mary Elizabeth being there. The doctors kept telling my wife and daughter that the prognosis was not good. My right side was totally paralyzed and my speech was very impaired. Surely, I thought, there must be an easier way to recover. Death was my other choice, but death, as someone once told me, is nature's way telling you to slow down.

I survived the stroke, and the aftermath of my long recovery only because of Dona's continuous support and help. In fact, I was able to not only survive the stroke but also to improve to the point of being able to complete this book.

Postlude

Pat Mendoza died August 22, 2012, after experiencing his second intracranial strokes. His stoke occurred on our 26th wedding anniversary. Fortunately, he and Jan Therkildsen had almost finished the book. Thank you to the publisher, ABC-CLIO, for giving me the opportunity to complete the manuscript and to you, the reader, for walking with our many veterans.

Dona Mendoza

Introduction

I was born from Irish and Cuban ancestors. I guess that makes me "Leprechano," and that would account for my love of stories.

I grew up in my father's shadow. Those of us who grew up in the late 1940s and 1950s, "baby boomers," all wanted to be just like our dads. We were taught in school what these men did for us. They saved not only our country but also the world from the likes of Hideki Tojo and Adolf Hitler

World War II was black and white to us, as it hit the movie screens and, then later, television screens with *Victory at Sea* and the *World at War*. But to the veterans, it was always in full, bloody color. And to my young child's eye, the men who fought these wars were giants. Their sweat and pain were seen in the face of every wounded veteran who lived in the housing project where I grew up.

We were taught the value of hard work and honesty; and we were taught to treat people the way you wanted to be treated. We were also taught that you took responsibility for your actions.

When I was in high school, I heard history names of the Boston Tea Party, Bunker Hill, and Paul Revere and the excitement of his midnight ride. But these stories didn't mean much to me until I left my home in Denver, Colorado, and embarked on my own adventures.

My exposure to the outside world lay dormant until I was awakened by a knock on my door from my neighbor. I was on my way to boot camp after joining the U.S. Navy in October 1964. There he stood, our 75-year-old neighbor, Mr. Handley. My mother assumed he was there to accuse me of something and assured him that everything was fine. For the past few years I had been a troublemaker. What really surprised me was his message.

His extended his right arm and he whispered "God speed. I know you will find peace. Patrick, I know you don't know much about me but I was in the great war . . . 1918 . . . War to end all Wars."

He then reminded me that his neighbor was a Civil War veteran. I realized then that I would share a deep connection with Mr. Handley, and with all other veterans. I will never forget Mr. Handley. He died just a month later. His words have for many years made me think of wars, their causation, and the many who have fought in them.

Soon after I began my quest to learn about history. I began reading and researching to find out more. In November 1780, the legend of Francis Marion was born when he created a fighting force known as Marion's Brigade. I had always thought that the Revolutionary War took place only in New England. I was shocked to find out that the last four battles of the Revolutionary War were fought in the Carolinas.

The swamps of South Carolina are a long way from Bunker Hill. As the crow flies it's just short of a thousand miles. South Carolina's low country receives almost no snow, while Massachusetts' snowfall can be devastating in its severity. This was history I had not learned in school.

As I continued reading and learning, I learned that history books can be somewhat misleading. According to some history texts, the last time America was invaded was by the British. However, Poncho Villa raided Columbus, New Mexico, in 1916, which was the first attack on U.S. soil since 1812. In the early morning hours of March 9, 1916, the town and its security changed forever.

Twenty-five years later, on December 7, 1941, American territory of Hawaii was attacked by the Japanese. Less than a year later, on June 3, 1943, Japan attacked and invaded off the coast of another American territory, the islands of Kiska and Attu in the Aleutian Islands, Alaska.

Two years before the U.S. involvement in Vietnam ended, and three years after I left the military, I worked as a deputy sheriff in Boulder County, Colorado. On May 23, 1971, I was thrown in head-first dealing with the Boulder riots for three days and nights. Antiwar chants and signs were everywhere. A Molotov Cocktail was thrown at me from Broadway Street in the area of town known as the "Hill." In conjunction with the riots, nightly television news continued showing film footage of the Vietnam War. One friend of mine in Tennessee watched the news every night, hoping to catch a glimpse of her husband in Vietnam. It was incredibly frustrating to me to have to deal with those protesting the war and disrespecting Vietnam veterans, when I knew of so many heroes, like Jim Goss (Chapter 17) who served with such high honor. Yet over time, I learned to work with people in a different way. I became a storyteller.

History is ever changing in its scope and technology. To live in freedom requires great sacrifice. I have become a listener to all religions and I have learned to share stories with the world's cohabitant humans instead of bullets.

There is magic in the word, written language, if only we take the time to speak carefully and to listen.

So, herein lies a collection of stories that I have collected over the years about individuals who have served in wars from the American Revolution through the Iraq War. They are meant to inform and entertain—to give human faces to the individuals involved in our country's wars. They are meant to provide other storytellers with stories they can share and retell; to be read by students of history who are looking for the stories of people behind history; and to be used by educators to supplement curricular units. They are organized chronologically, from the Revolutionary War (Bunker Hill) to Afghanistan and Iraq (Baghdad), with at least one story representing every war in our country's history. Many of the stories in this book are based on the recollections of individuals, which may or may not match recollections or accounts by others.

The more recent stories in this collection were primarily collected from personal interviews of the people involved in the stories, or from their living relatives. The historical stories were gathered from reading and research. Sources for the stories are listed by chapter at the end of this book.

Before leaving my doorstep, Mr. Handley offered one more piece of advice that I have always remembered.

> I made more than my share of mistakes in life, but the moral compass that was set out for me so long ago has always guided me back from where I had strayed.

As a professional storyteller and historian I have collected stories from four cultures. As a veteran, I have been especially interested in military stories. All the stories in this collection are fact based; and in my tellings, I have made every effort to aptly represent the truth. Some of these stories and their characters will be familiar to you; and some you may have never heard before, because throughout our history, many stories have been overlooked. These stories represent my own moral compass, and I hope through sharing them, I've added a little more understanding to our history.

Chapter 1

"The Devil Himself Could Not Catch Him": Francis Marion

Unless you've gone through public school in South Carolina, or you grew up in the mid-1950s watching "Walt Disney Presents," you may not have heard of Francis Marion. Francis Marion was a Revolutionary War Hero known as the "Swamp Fox," whose exploits became legend in the Deep South.

The swamps of South Carolina are a long way from Bunker Hill. As the crow flies it's just short of a thousand miles. However, both Boston and Charleston were major seaports and both played an important role in British wartime strategies of the American Revolution. But life in South Carolina was the antithesis of life in Massachusetts. The geography of the two states is similar in that they both have mountains, hills, farmland, and coastline; but the weather is far different —especially in winter. South Carolina's low country receives almost no snow, while Massachusetts's snowfall can be devastating in its severity.

On June 17, 1775, the first major battle of the Revolution took place just outside of Boston on the Charlestown Peninsula overlooking Boston Harbor. History claims the site as Bunker Hill, but the site of the actual fighting was the hill south of it named Breed's Hill. Though 1,500 American troops occupied both the hills, the actual first shots fired were on Breed's Hill. Those shots in Massachusetts started an all-out war that, over the next five years, was fought throughout the north in Pennsylvania, New Jersey, New York, and Connecticut in a hundred places and in all kinds of weather.

Breed's Hill and Bunker Hill were but a preview of the events to come. Though the British claimed their first victory, it had cost them sorely. More than 1,150 British soldiers were killed or wounded. The Americans lost 450 men either killed or wounded. Little did the British realize what lay ahead.

Life in the Low Country

The low country of South Carolina consists of vast fresh water rivers, marshes, and the sea. The rivers and marshes form large areas of swampland. Sea oat covers the sand dunes along the coastline, and the Atlantic Ocean runs warm with the Gulf Stream. Just inland, giant oak trees covered with Spanish moss create majestic canopies that lined the dirt roads from Camden to Charleston in 1775. There are a dozen or more islands that dot the coast all the way down to Georgia.

French Huguenots, British, and Scots Irish had settled the area, and left their imprint on the land. The introduction of slavery by the English dramatically changed the landscape and culture. Large plantations sprung up, and many a landowner became incredibly wealthy on the backs and minds of the slaves who worked for them.

One such story tells of an English sea captain who purchased a sack of rice from India for food. One of his slaves saw the rice and asked the man what he was going to do with it. His reply was "cook it and eat it." Because the slave had lived on the west coast of Africa where rice was a staple crop and food, he knew about rice. He convinced his "master" not to eat the rice but to let him plant it and grow it. This slave, as the story goes, grew the first rice crop in South Carolina, and ultimately created an unbelievable cash crop for Southern planters.

One such planter was Francis Marion. Though his parents were French Huguenots, Francis was born near Georgetown, South Carolina, in 1732. He was the youngest of six children, and as a boy, he loved to explore the swamps. After watching the ships that came in and out of Georgetown's port, Marion dreamed of a life at sea.

When he turned 15, Francis signed up as the sixth crewman of a schooner headed for the West Indies. On their return trip, the schooner collided with a whale, which caused a plank from the keel to loosen. The schooner immediately began taking on water in a leak that couldn't be stopped. The captain and crew abandoned their ship on a small lifeboat. The schooner sank so quickly that Marion and his mates were not even able to secure what food and water remained below decks. Six days later floating in the ocean on that lifeboat under the hot tropical sun, their luck began to run out. Two crewmen died of thirst and exposure. Francis was luckier. The following day, he and the rest of the men with him floated ashore. This adventure ended Marion's fascination with ocean travel; and he never returned to sea. However, Francis led a a charmed life.

Marion returned home, and stayed there for another six years. When he turned 21, he joined his brother Gabriel's militia. While fighting in the French and Indian War in 1753, he became a skilled soldier and an expert marksman.

After the war, Marion returned to South Carolina's low country to farm, but only until the Cherokee War outbreak in 1760. During the year of fighting,

Marion again demonstrated superior leadership skills and excelled as a cavalry-man. Horsemanship and being a good shot were vital skills in Indian warfare. The Cherokee were skilled warriors who were fighting for their very survival; and during this time, Marion learned a lot from them about guerilla-type warfare.

Back home, Marion and other planters grew crops such as hemp, flax, indigo, and tobacco. All of these "cash crops" made South Carolina one of the most prosperous colonies in the English empire. When the American Revolution broke out, losing was not acceptable to the British. However, after the initial rebellion in the North, the idea of independence quickly spread to the Southern colonies. England now faced keeping the peace in an area four times the size of England.

The Revolution Moves South

After their costly victory over the American troops at Bunker Hill, the British knew they had a real fight on their hands. Yet, they still felt that a quick campaign in their Southern colonies would be easy. They banked on local support, not realizing the extent of the opposition the South held.

Meanwhile, as an elected member of the Provincial South Carolina Congress in 1775, Francis voted for this country's independence. He then volunteered and was appointed captain of the 2nd South Carolina Regiment.

One year after the Battle of Bunker Hill, the British attempted to invade Charleston, South Carolina. The English thought that quick subjugation of the South could only strengthen their ranks and would leave them to deal with New England and Virginia.

They were wrong. Opposition to the British, particularly in South Carolina, swelled. Troops commanded by British Major General Henry Clinton attempted to land his troops in Charleston. Not knowing the waterways and tide flows, or the temperament of American patriots, proved his undoing.

American forces led by Colonel William Moultrie positioned themselves at Fort Sullivan, just north of Charleston, exchanged canon fire with British ships. One of the Americans fighting with Moultrie was Colonel Francis Marion. The accuracy of the American troops forced the English to retreat. They sailed north and remained out of South Carolina for the next four years.

In 1779, when the British again invaded the South, they did so with overwhelming forces and naval superiority. At first, patriot troops proved no match. American officers like Virginia's Light Horse Henry Lee and William Washington were nearly captured in numerous incidents, as the British began their northern march to clear South Carolina of its "traitors." Francis Marion himself barely evaded capture when the City of Charleston surrendered to the British in 1780. The month before Charleston's surrender, Marion broke his ankle while jumping from a second-story window to escape British troops.

Later that year, Marion again proved an exemplary officer in multiple raids on British troops in places like Great Savannah, Blue Savannah and Black Mingo Creek, and Tearcoat Swamp. Only when he hit Georgetown were British troops able to force him to retreat.

A Legend Is Born

Then, in November 1780, Francis Marion improvised and created a fighting force known as Marion's Brigade, and a legend was born. Snow's Island became headquarters for his guerilla band of fighters.

South Carolina winters were far different from those experienced by George Washington's troops in the north. The temperatures were cool, not frigid, but the swamps were incredibly dangerous to anyone, even those who knew them, if they were careless. Marion, like most of his men, knew the swamps of the area intimately. They were keenly aware that in the winter months, snakes and other reptiles hibernated, which meant that the risk of being bitten by copperheads and water moccasins at that time of year was minimal. Winter also meant that there were no mosquitoes or other insects. With this knowledge, they dared to roam swamp areas the British would never traverse.

Francis Marion was 48 years old and had recently been promoted to Brigadier General. By no means a young man, he had twice the stamina of those under his command. Marion was a stern disciplinarian and demanded the highest standards of military efficiency; and yet he was also kind and humane, sympathetic to the suffering of his ill-equipped men. He endured all that they suffered, including sleeping without tents or any other kind of shelter from the weather and cold. He never took unnecessary risks, though many of his bold actions took even the most experienced British officers by surprise. So Marion's devoted men followed him without question.

Marion rode in and around the rivers and swamps above Charleston to just south of the North Carolina border. British troops commanded by Lieutenant Colonel Banastre Tarleton were a favorite target. Tarleton had become the most hated and feared British officer in all of the Carolinas. Tarleton held no respect or honor for anyone in South Carolina. He and his elite cavalry unit known as the Green Dragoons terrorized not only colonial troops but also South Carolina's citizens. Tarleton routinely executed many of the "rebels" he captured. To give "quarter" in battle means to spare the enemy combatants who surrender. When fighting in the Waxhaw, North Carolina, Tarleton's men butchered American forces who tried to surrender after laying down their arms. This practice of cold-blooded murder became known as "Tarleton's Quarter" and would not be forgotten by American fighters. Marion harassed and attacked Tarleton whenever he could.

Unlike Tarleton, Marion didn't believe in savagery or cruelty. His second in command and best friend, Peter Horry wrote of him. "He not only prevented cruelty in his own presence, but strictly forbade it in his absence" (South Carolina Historical Society, Horry, 1842).

Even when savage acts were committed against members of his family, Marion would not tolerate a cruel revenge. For example, while traveling through Winya Bay, Marion's nephew, young Lieutenant Gabriel Marion along with a companion, Francis Goddard stumbled on a group of Tories. Both sides opened fire, and Marion's and his companion's horses were killed. Goddard escaped, but young Marion was captured. When the Tories began clubbing him with their rifle butts, an acquaintance of Gabriel's tried to intervene. The enraged Tories literally tore young Gabriel from his protector when they heard his name being mentioned.

One of the Tories screamed, "He is the breed of that damned old rebel!" He then put the barrel of his rifle to young Marion's chest and pulled the trigger firing a load of buckshot through his body. According to a witness, "The rifle shot was planted so near that it burnt the linen at his breast" (South Carolina Historical Society, Jenkins, 1842).

In revenge for Gabriel's murder, one of Marion's men executed a Tory who he believed was present at young Marion's death. When Francis Marion heard the report, he became infuriated and upbraided the man responsible with a severe tongue lashing and reprimand Peter Horry later wrote, "Of all the men who ever drew a sword, Marion was the most humane" (South Carolina Historical Society, Horry, 1842).

The British stepped up their search for Marion with Tarleton at the lead. At one point, Marion and his men vanished into the waterways and cover of Ox Swamp. Knowing his men and horses were too tired to travel on after a six-hour pursuit, a frustrated Tarleton cried out, "But for this damned old fox, the devil himself could not catch him" (South Carolina Historical Society, Jenkins, 1842) The story spread; and from then on, both the British and the Americans called Francis Marion the "Swamp Fox."

The frustrated Tarleton now began a reign of terror on the population of South Carolina. He burned and pillaged towns and homes. In one case, Tarleton rode to General Richard Richardson's plantation in Clarendon County. The colonial general had passed away six weeks before. Tarleton ordered the general's widow and servants to make dinner for him and his staff, insisting that the widow and children of General Richardson would pay for his deeds of revolt. They dined, drank, and took what they wanted from the house.

On November 9, Francis Marion described what happened next in a letter to General Horatio Gates:

> Colonel Tarleton has burnt all the houses, and destroyed all the corn, from Camden down to Nelson's Ferry. He has behaved to the poor women with great barbarity; beat Mrs. Richardson, a relict of General Richardson, to make her tell where I was, and not left her a change

of raiment. He not only destroyed all the corn, but burnt a number of cattle in the houses he fired. It is distressing to see women and children sitting in the open air without a fire, without a blanket, or any clothing but what they had on, and women of family, that had ample fortunes, for he spares neither Whig nor Tory." (South Carolina Historical Society, Marion, 1842)

Though disputed by some historians, one story persists in the low country of South Carolina, that while attempting to coerce information out of General Richardson's widow, Tarleton forced her to dig up her husband's grave. He then had her prop his body up in a chair. According to this story, Tarleton and his officers verbally disrespected General Richardson's corpse and his wife, before burning the plantation house down.

Further Adventures of the Swamp Fox

Meanwhile, Marion continued to harass Tarleton and the British. His daring raids were carried out at midnight; and he would vanish into the swamps before the British could reorganize and chase him. Many of his raids were designed to free colonists who had been taken prisoners.

In all of the raids and battles he planned and executed, Francis Marion was never defeated. The same could not be said about some of the battles that were planned by others in which he participated.

General Horatio Gates was a prime example. Three years earlier, when he defeated English General John Burgoyne and forced his army to surrender in Saratoga, New York, Gates had been hailed a hero for his victory. Slighting George Washington and his authority, the Continental Congress ordered Gates to South Carolina, where he now commanded all the Southern forces.

Gates sent written orders to Francis Marion, commanding him to join his troops. In their first meeting with Gates, Marion did not sit well with Gates. He took one look at the condition of Marion and his men and found them so shabby that he thought they would be a distraction to the regular troops. Gates wasted no time in ordering Marion and his troops out of camp to scout out British movements. He also sent away a brilliant cavalry commander out of camp, Lieutenant Colonel William Washington, George Washington's first cousin, because Gates thought cavalry would be of no use in South Carolina's terrain.

Gates's arrogance condemned him into ignominy in the Battle of Camden, South Carolina. He made classic military blunders in splitting his forces and sent some of his best troops away. The British routed Gates and sent 2,000 of his 3,000 men running without firing a single shot. Gates soon followed and within 10 hours rode his horse 60 miles north to Charlotte, North Carolina. Some 800 Americans were killed, wounded, or captured.

Horatio Gates was removed from command and he never commanded another combat brigade. He spent the remainder of the war in an office.

General George Washington replaced Gates with his longtime and trusted friend General Nathanial Greene. Greene, who hailed from Rhode Island, had served mostly in a noncombatant role. However, he was active in the Battle of Monmouth and was ready to fight. Greene turned out to be a brilliant and incredible military tactician, which in itself was remarkable, considering he was brought up a Quaker. Unlike Gates, Greene listened to his soldiers, particularly Francis Marion, and sought their advice about local geography. This was especially important because Greene's forces were fewer in number than British general Charles Cornwallis's troops. The plan he formed kept the many rivers and streams between his troops and the British. In fact, by adopting a larger version of Marion's hit-and-run tactics, Greene succeeded in a series of victories for the Americans.

In the Battle of Eutaw Springs, Greene drove the British off; and his victory broke the morale of the local Tories, who realized this was the beginning of the end. To paraphrase an old military saying, "Greene let Cornwallis chase him until Greene caught him."

Throughout this time, Francis Marion continued his assaults, hitting the British whenever he could. He often fought independently in his hit and-run style, much to the dismay of the British who were unable to catch or trap him. He also fought with Nathaniel Greene's troops and with Colonel Light Horse Harry Lee.

War Comes to an End

On January 17, 1781, the Battle of Cowpens took place near the North Carolina border. American troops commanded by General Daniel Morgan devastated British troops and Colonel Banastre Tarleton in a brilliant plan that brought the first major victory to the Southern campaign. The ferocity of the fighting became so intense that at one point American troops started bayoneting British troops who were trying to surrender, all the while yelling, "Tarleton's quarter!" Fortunately for the British, American officers stopped the carnage.

Francis Marion was not present at Cowpens. He was 200 miles south with Colonel Lee; and on January 24, they unsuccessfully attacked Georgetown, South Carolina. After the Battle of Cowpens, the British headed north. Tarleton escaped harm, and rejoined Cornwallis in his march to Virginia.

On October 19, 1781, Cornwallis and his army surrendered to General George Washington in Yorktown, Virginia, effectively bringing about the end of the American Revolution. However, even though Cornwallis surrendered, fighting continued for another year.

Francis Marion's last action of the war took place on the banks of the Cooper River, near Charleston. His small band of 80 men ambushed 200 British dragoons. Marion and his men opened fire and killed 20 men. Then Marion lost his ammunition wagon and could not continue the fight for lack of ammunition. Had he not lost that wagon, there truly would have been a slaughter of British troops. Marion withdrew, and again vanished to where the British could not find him.

After fighting for almost 10 years in the American Revolution, Francis Marion returned to Saint John's Parrish and began rebuilding his war-ravished home.

Story Notes

I never knew much about Francis Marion until I lived in South Carolina back in the late 1970s. His stories abounded throughout all the areas I roamed—Myrtle Beach, Conway, Spartanburg, George Town, Charleston, the Santee and Pee Dee Rivers, and the swamps and coastline. I was amazed at just how many things were named in his honor including a college, a county, countless schools throughout the state, and a "Public Square" in the middle of historic Charleston, South Carolina. To this day many newborns are named in honor of Francis Marion.

Marion is one of South Carolina's greatest heroes. During the years from 1776 until 1780 Francis Marion and his men were literally the only force that fought against the British.

*As a storyteller, one of the great treasures I found in 1980 was a wonderful oral historian and resident of Murrell's Inlet, South Carolina, 92-year-old Mr. Clark Wilcox. He told me the story about the slave growing rice in the low country. I remained in touch with Mr. Wilcox for five years and in 1985 when he was 97, he allowed me to film at his 157-year-old house and then sat with me for a lengthy video interview. Prior to my meeting with Mr. Wilcox, I read as much as I could about Francis Marion in the South Carolina Historic Society in Charleston; and then found one of the very few books published about him at that time—*The Swamp Fox *by Robert D. Bass. Since then, there have been at least two dozen books and even more articles published.*

*I still have the book—*The Swamp Fox. *The author, the late Dr. Bass, was one of the nation's leading scholars on the American Revolution.*

I also recommend Dr. Bass's biography of Banastre Tarleton, The Green Dragoon, *Sandlapper Publishing Company, paperback edition, 2003.*

In today's world, much of this information is available on the Internet through the State of South Carolina and historic societies; but I still prefer wandering through the hallways of libraries, museums, and state archives.

Chapter 2

The Voodoo Queen and the Pirate: Marie Leveau and Jean Lafitte

Veterans aren't always uniformed military personnel. In the War of 1812, citizen soldiers from every walk of life fought against the British, including Marie Leveau, a voodoo queen and Jean Lafitte, a pirate. Both fought against the British and helped Andrew Jackson win the Battle of New Orleans in January 1815.

Outside of New Orleans, the name of Marie Leveau may not be very familiar; yet hers is probably one of the most well-known names in the city. Leveau, the most famous voodoo queen in the Crescent City operated out of its famed French Quarter. In 1815, when just a teenager (around 14–19 years old), she purportedly used her unique talents to serve the American cause in the classic Battle of New Orleans. Or so the story goes.

Most lay accounts say she was born between 1794 through 1801 with "mystical" powers. Those who knew her said that she was a striking beauty of mixed blood, a white father and a Creole mother. Many said that her mystical powers came from a combination of her Roman Catholic beliefs, beliefs in the saints, African spirits, and her personal religious concepts. Some even said she had the ability to cast spells on her enemies. Whatever the case, in her lifetime, Marie Leveau was able to weave a phenomenal web of intrigue, herbal cures, and love potions, and ultimately make a powerful impact on history.

Leveau is not alone in this tale of unconventional war veterans. Another equally strange ally of the American troops was the pirate Jean Lafitte. Many say that without his help in procuring powder, ammunition, and manpower, General Andrew Jackson would not have defeated the invading British forces coming up the Mississippi Delta.

The Battle of New Orleans was the very last action of the War of 1812. In fact, the war had been over for two weeks when the battle took place. Because of incredibly slow communications, both the British and the Americans were unaware that the Treaty of Ghent had been signed to end the hostilities that began in 1812.

The United States had declared war on England for a variety of reasons. One was that the British Navy drafted over 10,000 American sailors since 1801, after searching and seizing U.S. ships without any cause or provocation. Other factors for the declaration involved the British claims in northern territories, and their arming of Native Americans, who were also at war with the United States. President Madison resolved to prevent an alliance between the British and Native Americans.

Within two years, in 1814, about 4,000 British troops marched on our nation's capital. At that time Washington, D.C., was surrounded by marshlands. American troops were quickly routed, and President Madison, who was with them, fled the area. When hearing of the British march on the White House, First Lady Dolly Madison quickly grabbed what valuables she could carry. One object she rescued was a full-length portrait of George Washington that she literally tore from the wall. Then, she and her staff quickly made their escape across the Potomac River.

That evening the British sacked the town destroying everything of value, including dockyards, the Senate House, warehouses, and barracks that housed 2,000 soldiers. Then they set the White House ablaze. The fire lit up the Virginia sky and the glow of the destruction could be seen for miles.

On August 25, 1814, shortly after the British attempted to settle in Washington, a powerful thunderstorm hit the city. Both legend and history claim that the storm spawned a huge tornado. Some say it was heard before it was seen as it roared into the city. When the twister hit, it ripped through the center of the city and touched down directly on British troops. What few buildings remained were torn off their foundations, trees were uprooted, and a heavy chained bridge that crossed the Potomac buckled. Flying debris killed many British soldiers. Others died when they could not escape the powerful winds.

Some believed that the storm was a divine intervention, as it caused the British to abandon Washington; it killed more British soldiers than had been killed in the battle.

The following month, Francis Scott Key gave birth to this country's national anthem when he witnessed the bombardment of Fort McHenry near Baltimore, Maryland, while being detained on a British ship. After seeing that the fort's large American flag was still fluttering in the wind after 25 straight hours of bombardment, he penned "The Star-Spangled Banner."

The fighting then moved south. The British reasoned that if they could take over the seaport at New Orleans, they could control the Mississippi River and all commerce that traversed the great river. Always an important port, New Orleans was the richest city in America at this time.

General Andrew Jackson, "Old Hickory" was ordered to defend the city to prevent such a move. Jackson commanded a small and poorly armed troop; and they were about to go up against 11,000 crack British troops. This time there would be no divine intervention.

The general sorely lacked powder and shot for his troops; and his lack of knowledge of the bayou country didn't help in planning the forthcoming fight. Local politics also hampered Jackson. Coming to Jackson's aid, though, was a teenaged voodoo practitioner and a wanted pirate.

Long before Jackson's arrival in New Orleans, a local Creole pirate named Jean Lafitte had established himself in the area, raiding English and Spanish vessels as well as some American ships during the Napoleonic War. Lafitte headquartered himself in and literally ruled the small island of Grande Terre and the Bay of Barataria near the mouth of the Mississippi River.

The governor of the State had offered a 500-dollar reward to anyone who captured the daring and audacious pirate. Five hundred dollars was a lot of money in 1814. However, when Lafitte heard the news about the reward, he didn't panic or worry about someone trying to hunt him down. What he did in response absolutely infuriated the governor. He posted a $5,000 reward for the capture of the governor and his delivery to Lafitte's hideout in Barataria!

However, fate eventually brought a cease to these two men's hostilities. That came in the name of General Andrew Jackson. Jackson had only been in New Orleans for about two weeks trying to find all of the supplies he and his men would need, and more importantly the right position to defend the city. In his search, he came upon the famous pirate.

When Jackson and Lafitte finally met, the two men struck a deal. In return for Lafitte's help in fighting the British, he and his men would be given full pardons. While Jackson prepared for the British march on the city, Lafitte and his crew sailed to Barataria and loaded their ships with powder, shot, cannons, and rifles.

Meanwhile, from her hairstyling shop, Marie Leveau listened to all the conversations her customers had with each other. Many of them confided in Marie. They trusted her, because in Marie's time in history, hairdressers did so much more than styling and cutting hair. They acted as midwives, pulled teeth, stitched wounds, and lanced boils. Marie did even more than that, though. Though just a teen, she was wise beyond her years. And she'd been schooled not only in herbal medicines but also in voodoo.

Voodoo, based on African religious beliefs and customs, had spread to Haiti and then on to New Orleans through the slaves. Leveau subscribed to its teachings, and also played off people's ignorance and superstitions. At that time, many people believed that a voodoo priestess could control time and the weather, as well as bring the dead back to life in the form of zombies.

Marie used a bit of sleight of hand to convince many of her magical powers. She made and sold potions for anything her customers asked. There were potions for whatever ailed you, and for anything or anyone you desired. Her practices weren't widely advertised, though, as the practice of voodoo was still punishable by death; and public executions were common. (People would even bring a picnic to the events, and often bet on how quickly the victim would die.)

Leveau heard tales of British cruelty, and how their victory would change life as she knew it. Marie wasn't ready for any changes, for she'd grown to love the open and free lifestyle of the "Big Easy." Her business was located in the lucrative French Quarter; and she was well acquainted with the New Orleans' elite as well as the middle class and poor people. All of them from time to time asked Marie for advice and other favors. So, Marie began sending her messengers and spies out into the bayou country to track British troop movements.

To Andrew Jackson, the most important thing Marie provided was an intelligence network with all of the other hairdressers in the city. Leveau rewarded them for lucrative information. All the hairdressers had access to all of their customers' homes while performing their non-hair-related duties. They overheard private conversations, as many of the customers considered the hairdressers as nonconsequential. Though free, they were, after all, black.

Marie regularly and secretly supplied Jackson with information as to who was loyal to the Americans and to those whose loyalties lay with the British. Other information came from a man Jackson was poised to hang, had he been given the chance. That man was Jean Lafitte.

The year before Jackson's arrival in New Orleans, the British tried to bribe Lafitte to gain his help in attacking the city. The pirate refused, but forwarded the information to New Orleans officials, who promptly ignored it. A few weeks later, a small British fleet attacked the port city. They did not immediately come ashore or invade. Confident that conquering New Orleans would be relatively easy, many of the British officers had actually brought their wives along in the transports, so they could shop in New Orleans after the battle. (The women of New Orleans were believed to be not only exotic and beautiful but also great lovers of fashion and jewelry, so the port town had become a shopping destination for the British.)

Meanwhile, Jackson had been suffering from a bout of dysentery and lead poisoning from a bullet lodged in his shoulder from a Nashville street brawl with political enemies two years before. However, he and his troops managed to fortify the city and awaited reinforcements. They finally arrived just days before the actual fight for the city. Old Hickory, as Jackson was called, immediately put his focus on touring New Orleans to determine what was needed to strengthen defenses. He put men to work blocking the many bayous that the enemy might use. Jackson vowed to himself that the British would not prevail. His deep hatred for them stemmed from when he was a teenager. He and his brother had been taken prisoner during the Revolutionary War; and when

Jackson refused to shine an officer's boot, he was struck in the hand and fore-head with a blow from a saber that left him scarred for life.

Jean Lafitte delivered ammunition, cannons, shot, and powder to Jackson's greatly outnumbered army. The troops were made up of a small number of U.S. soldiers, Tennessee and Kentucky Volunteers, New Orleans militia, local Indi-ans, and local plantation owners. It was said that even a contingent of former Haitian slaves who were now free men took up arms that morning to fight under the stars and stripes. Some sources assert and others deny that Lafitte and his men were there with Jackson in the middle of the battle.

In the early morning hours of January 8, 1815, Jackson's defenders heard the drumming of the British soldiers as they marched toward the city. According to some accounts, there was a light fog that morning, which worsened when the shooting started. In any case, the gun smoke became so thick that it covered the morning light. Fortunately for Jackson, the poor British leadership and swampy terrain, along with his troops' tenacity created a disastrous and embarrassing defeat for the British.

In less than an hour of fighting, the British surrendered to Jackson. About 300 British men were killed and another 1,200 wounded, while on the Ameri-can side only 13 were killed and 52 wounded.

During the battle, Marie Leveau brought her healing skills to the battlefield and nursed many of the wounded. Not yet 20 years old, Marie Leveau's herbal knowledge surpassed that of most doctors of the time. She packed tree moss into many of the soldiers' wounds to prevent infections. (Tree moss contains the same healing ingredients as that of penicillin.)

One eyewitness account stated that when the smoke cleared the battlefield looked like a "sea of blood." It was the combination of the British red coats lying on the ground mixed with the blood of the dead and wounded. Where Brit-ish columns had stood, the ground was now, "entirely covered with prostrate bodies" (*Louisiana Historical Quarterly*, 1926).

Thanks to an unlikely duo—a voodoo queen and a pirate, the Battle of New Orleans became a huge victory for the United States; and it made Andrew Jackson a larger-than-life figure.

Fourteen years later, Jackson was elected the seventh president of the United States. Jackson has been both revered and hated in American history, depending on one's beliefs. Many Native Americans detested Jackson's forced removal of the Cherokee Nations during his presidency. The march from the Carolinas to what is now the State of Oklahoma is known as the "Trail of Tears." Thousands died. Yet, Jackson was also the only president in the history of the United States to pay off the national debt.

Jean Lafitte and his men were pardoned for all of their crimes, and he even-tually left Louisiana. Some stories say that he sailed toward Galveston, Texas, where he resumed his pirate ways. No one really knows how he died. There are many stories about it, ranging from his being killed in a hurricane to his moving to Saint Louis and living there until around 1826. As with Marie Leveau, very little documentation exists about her life.

However, Lafitte is well remembered in New Orleans folklore and has always been romanticized as a gallant and cavalier swashbuckler. Though offered a small fortune to fight for the British, according to the tales, he turned it down because he believed in the concepts of democracy. Of course, no one knows for sure what his motives were.

As for Marie Leveau, like Lafitte, she became a living legend. She married and was said to have had 15 children, many of them sets of twins. She purportedly continued operating from her hairdressing shop in the French Quarter for most of her life.

Those who witnessed Leveau's voodoo rituals said that they involved her amidst hundreds of snakes, including all four varieties of poisonous snakes indigenous to Louisiana—rattlesnake, copperhead, cottonmouth or water moccasin, and coral snake. However, much of her power also came from superstition, fear, and intimidation.

No one knows for sure the year she died, but it is rumored that it was 1881 or 1897, when she would have been very old. Some say she was 105 years old when she died. After her death, there were reports of Marie being seen alive, looking much younger than her years. This story was likely prompted by the sight of or even propagated by one of her many daughters, who bore uncanny resemblances to their mother.

Marie Leveau's burial place is just one more in a hundred mysteries about the famous voodoo queen. Many say that she is buried in Glapion Tomb or Saint Louis Number One. Yet, to add to the mystery, one of Marie Leveau's daughters was also named Marie, and she too was a voodoo queen.

Story Notes

I first heard stories of Marie Leveau and Jean Lafitte in New Orleans a few days before the 1970 Mardi Gras celebration. As I roamed the streets of the French Quarter, I listened, not only to the great jazz, but also to the great stories the city offered. I also had the chance to visit what are reported to be Marie Leveau's gravesites including the Glapion and Number One tombs in New Orleans.

Years later in September 2005, my friend, Faye Wooden, a wonderful storyteller from Tennessee, invited me to perform at a Red Cross Shelter that housed the victims of Hurricane Katrina. To my surprise, I was hardly given time to perform. Instead I spent hours listening to the stories that these victims chose to tell me. In a couple of instances, Marie Leveau's name came up and it was said that if she had been alive, she would have turned back the storm and floodwaters.

To this day, almost nothing is historically documented about either Leveau or Lafitte, but they are both very much alive in legend and folklore in one of America's most celebrated cities. Most of the stories about the Battle of New Orleans were oral, but the actual actions of that day are well documented by numerous history books, journals, and have actually been made into several fictitious movie accounts.

Chapter 3

For God? Or for Country?: John Riley and the San Patricios of the Mexican War

Ever since there has been war, there have been traitors. The most famous traitor in American history was Benedict Arnold. Had he not sold out to the British, his name would have been included as one of America's greatest military leaders. Instead, the very mention of his name is synonymous with treachery.

The following story is not about one traitor. It concerns 120 traitors. Many of these men, Irish immigrants, enlisted to serve their new country in time of war amidst prejudice and religious differences. The story of the San Patricios (Spanish for the "Saint Patricks") is almost unknown in American history books.

A long-running joke in England is "the capital of Ireland is Liverpool, England"; and in terms of population, this statement is true. There are actually more Irish living in Liverpool than in Dublin, Ireland!

The transformation of the English city began during the Great Potato Famine of 1845. Life had always been hard for the Ireland's rural population, but when an airborne fungus hit the land, it destroyed almost every potato crop in Ireland. Instead of a firm potato being dug up at harvest time, all that remained was a black gooey mess.

Of course, there were no pesticides available in the 19th century; and to make matters worse, most of the rural farmers didn't even own the land on which they worked. Their English overlords did little to help; the government too did not offer a safety net. By the time the famine ended, over a million Irish had died of starvation and disease. There are many people, including historians, as seen on the many episodes of the History Channel over the years, who claim this action was a deliberate act of genocide. Those capable of leaving immigrated to Liverpool to work in the shipyards and factories. Here they encountered incredible prejudices and discrimination, mainly on the grounds that they were Catholic. You see, since the time of Henry VIII, the Anglican Church had ruled England. Because the Catholic Church forbade Henry Tudor from divorcing his wife, Ann Boleyn, the king severed her head along with his ties with the Roman Catholic Church. He then created the Church of England, or the Anglican Church. Over the next 300 years the Catholics were slowly but brutally forced to convert, or face the consequences.

The Southern Irish refused to convert. Now, with thousands of these Catholic immigrants arriving in Liverpool, the city would never be the same. From this major seaport they began their immigration to the United States and Canada.

Within the next decade, several million Irish migrated to Great Britain, Canada, and the United States (Digital History website).Thousands did not survive the trip sailing across the Atlantic to the United States. Many were crammed into ships that were used by slave traders—into spaces that the slaves had been chained in. Diseases like cholera, dysentery, and small pox, as well as death by starvation, ravaged these passengers. So many people died during these voyages that sharks constantly followed these ships awaiting their next meal. The ships became known as "coffin ships."

Unfortunately, upon their arrival on American shores, the Irish were not welcomed with open arms.

Factory and waterfront signs greeted them with, "Irish need not apply." Or "No Irish." Few job opportunities were available to America's newest immigrants.

With the new arrivals came the loss of the culture they had left behind. Gaelic was rarely spoken in North America—English dominated in the new country.

The largest employer that a healthy young Irish man could find was the U.S. Army. The Army offered food, wages, clothing, and adventure. In fact, the U.S. Army had set up a recruitment center on Ellis Island to induce new immigrants into service. During the height of the Irish immigration, the United States had been at war with Mexico since 1841; and the country now needed new recruits to send to Mexico. Keep in mind that at the time of this war, Mexico included all of California, Arizona, New Mexico, Texas, the southern half of Colorado, and even parts of Utah and Kansas.

This latest war with Mexican bred new military leaders who awaited their destinies on history's grand stage. Among the most venerated to come of age were Robert E. Lee, Ulysses Simpson Grant, and future president of the Confederate States of America, Jefferson Davis.

Many of the Irish enlisted as soon as they stepped off the boat. They were quickly trained and shipped West to fight.

Mystery and legend surround one of the most famous of the Irish soldiers. Even his name is unclear. He was known under many names including John Riley, John Reilly, or John O'Reilly and was reportedly from County Galway, Ireland. Some claim he deserted the British Army in Canada and made his way south to the United States.

Some accounts say Riley was made a sergeant or sergeant major, and then sent to fight in the Mexican War. Being Irish and Catholic in the 1840s U.S. Army was not much easier than being Irish and Catholic in the Liverpool shipyards. There was a great deal of verbal and, at times, even physical abuse. Riley, though, could give back what he received in a fight. Throughout the history of the United States, the tenacity of Irish troops is legendary. They carried not only their valor into battle but also a motto that spread into every Irish community, "*Erin Go Bragh*," Gaelic for "Ireland Forever."

In 1846, an Irish regiment of American soldiers was ordered to join General Zachary Taylor's army and invade Mexico. This invasion brought about an incredible series of events that turned these American soldiers into Mexican patriots.

Nobody knows for sure why these soldiers deserted and began fighting on the other side. Historians differ in their opinions. Some say that many of the troops, including Sergeant John Riley became disillusioned with life in the U.S. Army, and their mistreatment and abuse from Anglo-Protestant officers. There were reports too that they witnessed uncontrolled rape, murder, robbery, and the desecration of Catholic Churches by Texas Rangers and other volunteers. It has also been said that John Riley's sympathies rested with the Mexican people, who like him, were Roman Catholic. Other reports state that many of these Irish soldiers were enticed to desert and join the Mexican Army, not because of religious kinships but for higher wages and Promised Land grants.

What *is* known is that about 120 Irish soldiers deserted the ranks of the U.S. Army and joined the Mexican Army. These men shared one thing with the Mexican Army: they were all Roman Catholic. And legend holds that John Riley became not only a willing participant in this mass desertion but also one of its leaders. He was reported to have deserted the U.S. Army in Matamoros, Mexico, in April 1846, before war was declared.

The Irish and Mexicans shared common histories of oppressors, who sought to destroy their cultures and religion. This tightened their bond even closer.

These men formed a battalion in the Mexican Army called the "San Patricios." The Mexican government commissioned Riley as captain of artillery.

Riley and his San Patricios first fought as a recognized Mexican unit in the Battle of Monterrey on September 21, 1846. One wonders what their battalion flag looked like, but legend has it that it was emerald green with images of a shamrock, an Irish harp, and Saint Patrick.

Their artillery skills repelled repeated American assaults into the heart of that city; but they were no match for the size and fighting abilities of the American army. Riley and his men lost this engagement, but the story of Monterrey spread. Soon after, the San Patricios grew in number to around 800 men. European Catholics who were living in Mexico and southern Texas volunteered to fight for their Catholic brethren. Their ranks grew with even more Irish desertions from the U.S. Army.

During the next few months, after joining a much larger force commanded by General Antonio López de Santa Ana, Riley and his men marched north.

The name Santa Ana was well known by the Americans. Santa Ana had no sympathy for the roughly 189 defenders of the Texas mission of the Alamo in 1836. Among those killed were William Travis, Jim Bowie, and Davy Crockett. There were no survivors except for the women who stayed, including Susannah Dickenson and her 15-month-old daughter Angelina.

This was the same Santa Ana who slaughtered 300 Texans in Goliad *after* they had surrendered. His fortune turned though on April 21, 1836, when he met Sam Houston in the Battle of San Jacinto. Houston's troops surprised Santa Ana and his men. In just a few hours, outnumbered two to one, Sam Houston and his men killed over 700 Mexican soldiers and captured another 750. Santa Ana himself was captured while trying to escape, disguised as a woman.

Now, nearly 10 years later Santa Ana again led a large army against the Americans. Among the U.S. troops, there were those present who remembered the Alamo and Goliad. When they discovered that Santa Ana commanded the Mexican troops, a new fervor for battle soon spread throughout the ranks.

In the next major engagement, the Battle of Buena Vista, Riley and his San Patricios were assigned the three largest cannons the Mexican Army possessed, and positioned themselves on the high ground overlooking the battle ground. Again, the San Patricios' artillery skills served the Mexican Army well. They repelled repeated charges on their position by the Americans attempting to capture the Mexican cannons.

In the heat of battle, Riley and his men counterattacked the American forces and captured two of their artillery pieces. For their heroic defense at Buena Vista, Riley and others were awarded the Mexican Medal of Honor. However, many of Riley's men were purportedly killed, and his battalion was greatly reduced in size.

Though heavily outnumbered, the American troops forced Santa Ana's army to retreat and won a hard-fought victory.

Riley and the San Patricios reorganized into an infantry unit but continued to serve with distinction. John Riley now commanded the first infantry company under Colonel Francisco Moreno as they marched to Cerro Gordo.

Knowing that they faced the death penalty if captured by the Americans, the San Patricios vowed to kill any Mexican soldier who tried to retreat from the battle. They simply had too much to lose. However, John Riley and the others could not carry out their threat because they were in hand-to-hand combat with the American forces, and many of the Mexican soldiers bolted and ran for their lives.

The luck of the Irish failed them in their next major engagement, the Battle of Convent Churubusco in Mexico City. The Spanish built the old convent in the 16th century. The convent became an important base of operations for the defense of Mexico City.

On August 20, 1847, fighting side-by-side with their Mexican brothers in arms, the San Patricios took to the high ground on the parapets of the Convent of Churubusco. After an especially cruel battle, the San Patricios, outnumbered and out of ammunition, continued fighting until they were shot down. Thirty-five lay dead and another 85 were wounded and captured, including John Riley. Another 80 plus men escaped with the retreating Mexican Army and fled to regroup, but they too had lost many men and one of their leaders.

Ironically, one of the American units that stormed the convent were the 1st New York Volunteers, made up almost entirely of Irish Catholics, commanded by 2nd Lieutenant Thomas W. Sweeney, from County Cork. He continued to fight even after being wounded in his right arm, which necessitated in having it amputated above the elbow.

Unsuccessful in their last fight, the San Patricios were officially discharged from the Mexican Army. John Riley and the others captured at Churubusco were not as lucky.

The U.S. Army tried and convicted the San Patricios as deserters and traitors. Their tenacity and ferocity in battle, in some of the toughest fighting in the war, thus far, were responsible for some of the heaviest U.S. casualties. Two separate court-martial trials were held; and at no time did military lawyers represent the San Patricios, as is custom. No transcripts were taken at either proceeding.

At this time, one common defense for deserters in military trials was drunkenness: a claim of "we wouldn't have done it if we'd been sober." Others claimed that they had been captured and forced to join the Mexican Army in one form or another. Neither Riley nor the vast majority of his company offered a defense for their actions.

Their sentence was death. By military law, the sentence would have been death by a firing squad. Military authorities decided that those condemned to die would not be shot but hanged.

Because John Riley's desertion took place before the declaration of war between Mexico and the United States, his trial and conviction were that of a deserter. He and 15 others were spared the death penalty but suffered the fate of all deserters.

The Army shaved Riley's and the other men's heads, and proceeded to drum them out of the army. Forced to stand at attention, the brass buttons on their uniforms were stripped off as well as any U.S. strips of rank. All of the men were then marched out of the fortress. All were given 50 lashes on their bare backs and then branded a two-inch, letter "D" on the right cheek with a hot iron.

Legend holds that John Riley was branded twice. Some say that the first brand was placed upside down on the left cheek by accident. He was then forced to endure the second correct placement of the brand on the right cheek. Some say that this was not an accident but an act of revenge.

After the war, Riley and the others were to be brought back to the United States; but the Mexican government intervened and the San Patricios remained in Mexico.

In 1850, 20 of the San Patricios left Mexico and returned to their native, Ireland. Legends regarding John Riley's fate abound. Some say he vanished into the hills and mountains of Mexico and was never seen again. There are also reports that Riley died in the last days of August in 1850. In fact, on a visit to Mexico some years ago, I saw a grave in the Vera Cruz cemetery that bears the name Juan Reley, which is the name John Riley used to enlist in the Mexican Army.

The desertion of the Irish troops was not an isolated occurrence during the Mexican War. More than 9,000 incidents of desertion occurred overall but only the San Patricios were punished so severely, including the mass hangings. In fact, until 1862, when 38 Dakota men were hanged en masse in Mankato, Minnesota, the execution of the 30 San Patricios was the largest mass execution in American history.

To this day, little is known as fact about all of the men who made up the San Patricio Battalion. There are military records documenting the existence of John Riley, even though there are numerous spellings of his names, including the one in Spanish on a headstone in Vera Cruz.

What is known though is that in 1915, the American War Department, now called the Department of Defense, acknowledged the San Patricios' existence as well as the ill treatment they received at the end of the Mexican War. Two years later, Congress ordered the war department to turn over their records to the National Archives. Complying with this order revealed what has become known as one of the most embarrassing episodes for the American army.

The Mexican people will forever remember the San Patricios. In 1997, Mexico officially recognized the contributions of the Irish through a commemorative postage stamp and other official acts. On October 28, 2002, the inscription in gold letters of "*Defensores de la Patria 1846–1848 de San Patricio,*" which translates to "the defenders of the fatherland and the San Patricio Battalion," was dedicated on the Wall of Honor in the Chambers of the Congress. Some 394 Mexican Congressman and Art Agnew, the Irish Ambassador to Mexico, attended the ceremony honoring the sacrifices made by the young Irish soldiers.

Ever since 1846, the Mexican people have honored these men in schools, churches, and other landmarks, such as street names. The street in front of the Convent of Churubusco was named "The Irish Martyrs." The street in front of the Irish School in suburban Monterrey is named "Battalion of Saint Patrick."

And to this day, two important dates in Mexico are remembered every year: One is September 12, the day the San Patricios were executed and the other is Saint Patrick's Day.

Historians widely differ on the details of many of the stories about the San Patricios, including whether their punishment fit the crime, but the question that remains in the minds of many are Were these men fighting for "God"? Or for "country"?

Story Notes

The Irish story is dear to anyone of Irish ancestry. My maternal grandmother, Maude Hanneghan was born in County Cork, and was orphaned as a small child. She lived in Liverpool for a while before immigrating to the United States in about 1900, when anti-Irish sentiments were still common. Tales of the Great Potato Famine were still being told then and retold down through the years to my mother and her siblings. My paternal great-great grandmother, Jennie Short, was also from County Cork; and eventually immigrated to New York where she lived during the Civil War. Again, family stories from her line were passed down through the generations about the great famine.

I first heard the story of the San Patricios many years ago when I was in Mexico City. Tourists are often caught up in the sights and sounds of the countries they visit, particularly the music. What caught my attention in Mexico, though, was not the sound of Mexican music but of Irish music. I was amazed. It was Saint Patrick's Day, but the last thing I expected to hear were the sounds of an Irish celebration. That's when I first heard the story of John Riley. Someone told me he was buried in coastal city of Vera Cruz. I traveled the roughly 120 miles and through the assistance of a local guide I located the headstone bearing the name of Juan Reley. I have never forgotten the story or the experience.

Some 28 years later I located numerous websites that substantiated what I had heard, and gave further details on the story of these men. Check the Sources at the end of this book for just a few.

Chapter 4

It All Started in His Front Yard:
Wilmer McLean

*Thousands of books have been written about the Civil War. There are far
too many unique and unusual stories to be compiled in just one book. But,
so many of that war's characters—its heroes and villains—wove circuitous
routes throughout its four years and left an indelible mark on history, as
well as on today's life. Many of the Civil War's generals went on to become
distinguished statesmen, educators—even president of the United States.
This tale, though, is about a simple farmer.*

In 1861, 47-year-old Wilmer McLean lived as a gentleman farmer in Northern Virginia. The retired major of the state militia owned a farm in Yorkshire
Plantation in Manassas, Virginia. He had heard rumors of war in his "country"
of Virginia for quite some time. And Major McLean was loyal and was ready to
fight, even though he considered himself too old for combat.

The events in America's West turned those rumors into reality. Kansas
drew first blood when the abolitionist John Brown took his followers to fight the
proslavery forces that had moved into the area. Then, in December 1859, John
Brown led a daring raid on the Union arsenal at Harpers Ferry in northwestern
Virginia. Colonel Robert E. Lee, then of the Union Army, was dispatched to
the scene with a company of U.S. Marines. The Marines assaulted the arsenal,
and within three minutes killed most of Brown's followers and captured him at
saber point.

Brown was tried, convicted, and hanged for treason in leading an armed
resurrection against the United States. But his actions were but a preview of the
horror of things to come.

Spectators at John Brown's hanging included a college professor, Thomas
J. Jackson, as well as a teenage actor named John Wilkes Booth.

Political differences between the Southern states and the Northern states escalated on two major issues: slavery and trade. The presidential elections ignited the fire that brought the simmering pot of hatred to a boil.

Abraham Lincoln's election as the 16th president of the United States on November 6, 1860, certainly escalated the events that led to the American Civil War, or as Wilmer McLean and others in the South called it, "The War of Northern Aggression." South Carolina had vowed to secede from the union if Lincoln was elected.

General David F. Jamison presided over the convention in which South Carolina chose to secede from the Union at 1:15 p.m. on December 20, 1860. That convention took place in Charleston, at Saint Andrews Hall, because of the smallpox epidemic in Columbia.

When James L. Petigrew, an eminent lawyer and unionist, heard Charleston's bell ringing in celebration of secession, he inquired where the fire was. When told there was no fire, he retorted, "I tell you there is a fire. They have, this day, set a blazing torch to the temple of Constitutional liberty, and we shall have no more peace" (*White River Valley Historical Quarterly,* 1969).

Within 10 days, cadets from Charleston's military academy, The Citadel, were among the troops occupying Morris Island, protecting the entrance of Charleston Harbor. Lieutenant Colonel John L. Branch commanded this fortification. The first two shots against the Union Army were fired by Citadel cadets G. E. Haynesworth of Sumter and C. S. Pickens, when they fired upon the USS *Star of the West*, which was attempting to send reinforcements and supplies to Fort Sumter in Charleston Harbor. Those shots forced the ship to turn back.

On February 4, 1861, the Confederate States of America came into being. Virginia's secession had incredible implications, for this state was considered home of the aristocracy of the South. Seven of the first 16 presidents of the United States were Virginians, including founding fathers George Washington, Thomas Jefferson, and James Madison. One of George Washington's best friends and another Revolutionary War hero, Light Horse Harry Lee, was also a Virginian. He was the father of Colonel Robert E. Lee, the brilliant military leader who led the raid to capture John Brown. Robert E. Lee was married to Mary Anna Custis Randolph, the adopted granddaughter of Martha Washington. Ironically, Lee opposed slavery and had freed the slaves he owned before the war broke out.

The secession of Lee's state brought consternation not only to him but also to almost every person in Virginia, including Wilmer McLean.

In a meeting at Blair House, the official presidential guesthouse, in Washington, D.C., Lee was asked by President Lincoln to take command of the Union Army. He turned the offer down, and resigned his commission in the U.S. Army. With the war imminent, Lee knew that he would have to invade Virginia. He could not bring it upon himself to lead an invading army into his own "country."

On April 12, 1861, confederate troops in Charleston, South Carolina, under the command of General P.T.G. Beauregard attacked the Union fortification of Fort Sumter in Charleston, South Carolina's harbor. Within two days the Union troops surrendered their fort.

Newspapers all over Virginia and the rest of the United States carried the news. Virginia became the site where the country plunged into its bloody Civil War.

Now, Brigadier General P.G.T. Beauregard's name didn't mean a lot to Wilmer MacLean until almost three months later. But the news of Confederate troops moving north was not a rumor. On July 21, Wilmer MacLean watched in awe, and with a twinge of horror, as thousands of Confederate troops gathered on his and the surrounding properties in Manassas.

Brigadier General Beauregard, the hero of Charleston, approached McLean and requested the use of his farmhouse as his temporary headquarters. Wilmer quickly agreed, thinking he would get a front row seat of the coming battle. Also gathered that day were 35,000 Union troops and dozens of Washington, D.C., citizens, all hoping to watch a quick Union victory over the Confederates. Many had brought picnic baskets. After the first shots were fired, no one there, including the soldiers, could believe what happened.

One of the first cannon balls fired hit Wilmer's house, then came down the chimney and destroyed the pot of stew that was intended for Beauregard and his staff. After that, it was pure mayhem.

Almost all of the Union soldiers were inexperienced and not very well disciplined. Shortly after the battle, Corporal Samuel J. English in Company D of the Second Rhode Island Volunteers described his experiences to his mother in a letter that read in part,

> On our arrival into the open field I saw I should judge three or four thousand rebels retreating for a dense woods, firing as they retreated, while from another part of the woods a perfect hail storm of bullets, round shot and shell was poured upon us, tearing through our ranks and scattering death and confusion everywhere; but with a yell and a roar we charged upon them driving them again into the woods with fearful loss. In the mean time our battery came up to our support and commenced hurling destruction among the rebels. As I emerged from the woods, I saw a bombshell strike a man in the breast and literally tear him to pieces. I passed the farmhouse, which had been appropriated for a hospital and the groans of the wounded and dying were horrible.
>
> I then descended the hill to the woods which had been occupied by the rebels at the place where the Elsworth zouaves [NOTE: Zouaves were U.S. troops whose flamboyant uniforms were fashioned to resemble North African troops with that name.] made their charge;

the bodies of the dead and dying were actually three and four deep, while in the woods where the desperate struggle had taken place between the U.S. Marines and the Louisiana zouaves, the trees were spattered with blood and the ground strewn with dead bodies. The shots flying pretty lively round me I thought best to join my regiment; as I gained the top of the hill I heard the shot and shell of our batteries had given out, not having but 130 shots for each gun during the whole engagement. As we had nothing but infantry to fight against their batteries, the command was given to retreat; our cavalry not being of much use, because the rebels would not come out of the woods.

The R.I. regiments, the New York 71st and the New Hampshire 2nd were drawn into a line to cover the retreat, but an officer galloped wildly into the column crying the enemy is upon us, and off they started like a flock of sheep every man for himself and the devil take the hindermost; while the rebels' shot and shell fell like rain among our exhausted troops.

("The First Battle of Bull Run, 1861,"
Eyewitness to History, 2004)

The college professor Thomas J. Jackson was now a Confederate colonel. At one point in the Battle of Bull Run, his troops held their line so effectively against charging Union troops that Confederate Brigadier General Barnard E. Bee said, "Jackson's troops stood like a stone wall." From that time on, Thomas J. Jackson was forever known as Stonewall Jackson.

In this first battle of the Civil War, the Union troops were slaughtered and humiliated. At the time, Wilmer could not have foreseen, nor could have anyone else, that the next four years would bring such rage and carnage to the country, but with the presence of Northern troops and the promise of more bloodshed near his home, Wilmer decided to leave. Another reason for his move was that Wilmer McLean, besides being a farmer worked as a Confederate sugar broker and conducted most of his business in southern Virginia. With his desire to be closer to work and to keep his family out of harm's way, Wilmer soon relocated more than 100 miles southwest of Manassas, Virginia.

Wilmer and his family lived in relative quiet during the next three years, while all around the war raged on with unbelievable carnage and rage.

To the west of him, the town of Winchester changed hands between Confederate and Union armies 73 times; while farther south and west in Tennessee near a country church called Shiloh, the South suffered a great loss. Tactically, the Northern Army under the command of General Ulysses S. Grant defeated a powerful Confederate Army commanded by General Albert Sidney Johnston and Brigadier General P.G.T Beauregard. But victory came at a price—Grant's casualties were horrendous. Over 13,000 Union soldiers were killed, wounded, or missing, while the Southern casualties were over 10,000. There had never been so many killed before in any battle. Ironically, the word "Shiloh" is a biblical term and it means "a place of peace."

The following August 28–29, slaughter again overwhelmed Wilmer's Manassas property in the Second Battle of Bull Run. And, again, Southern troops won the battle. Eighteen days after Robert E. Lee's victory, the general took his troops, north near the town of Sharpsburg, Maryland, near Antietam Creek. By this time, Lee's men were barefoot and lived off of green apples and corn. On September 17, he met General George McClellan's Northern troops. What transpired was one of the bloodiest single days in all of American history with 22,000 casualties. At one point in the battle, Confederate General John B. Hood ordered a courier to tell the soldiers on the field to charge. The courier returned and Hood asked, "Why aren't those men charging?" The courier answered, "Great God, general, they are all dead—there's nobody there to charge."

When the battle was over, Hood asked one of his officers, "Where is your division?" The officer answered, "Dead on the field" (Schreadley, 2012).

Casualties grew with each year as the war continued. From July 1 to 3, 1863, Lee's army invaded the northern state of Pennsylvania, near the little town of Gettysburg, in search of shoes and supplies for his men. Lee's troops again met McClellan's troops by chance; and in this, the greatest battle of the war, over 53,000 men were killed and wounded. (This toll in itself is amazing. In the 10 years of fighting in Vietnam over a hundred years later, 58,000 Americans were killed.)

Lee again escaped McClellan's army and made his way back to Virginia. The slaughter continued. At one point, the Union had to create burial places for the incredible numbers of dead. This task was assigned to Quartermaster General Montgomery Meigs, a southerner who came to hate the South. In 1864, General Meigs ordered that Robert E. Lee's home of Arlington be confiscated and turned into a military burial ground. Based on this recommendation, Arlington National Cemetery was created in that same year. Meigs, who knew Lee from the Mexican War, despised him for fighting for the South. Moreover, Meigs's son had been killed that same year; and Miegs decided to fill Arlington's land with the dead of those killed by the South. He intended that the land would forever be rendered uninhabitable. By the end of June, 2,600 bodies were interred.

Meanwhile, Wilmer McLean considered himself lucky in that the war had ravaged the lands and towns all around him in every direction but had not touched his new property. That would change. On Palm Sunday, April 9, 1865, McLean noticed an unusual number of Confederate troops in the town of Appomattox Courthouse, and all around his farm.

Confederate officers approached Wilmer, and questioned him about a suitable home or building they could occupy. One of the men asked about his home. Wilmer wasn't pleased about that. He remembered what had happened to his Manassas farmhouse. He remembered the cannonball that came down his chimney into his kettle of stew; and the screams of the dying still echoed in his ears.

Now with troops again wanting the use of his home, Wilmer inquired, "Why? Why my house?" He was not pleased as he watched his crops trampled and fences torn down. But the officers were courteous in their reply.

When General Robert E. Lee surrendered to General Ulysses S. Grant that day he found Wilmer's house to be the only one suitable. This shocked Wilmer McLean into silence. It also told Wilmer that the war was all but over. The commander of the Army of Northern Virginia was surrendering.

The Confederate troops now awaited the procedures. Wilmer looked on in amazement as Lee's troops, now starving and ill equipped to continue fighting, dug through horse manure for undigested corn to eat. They literally couldn't continue without being slaughtered.

Robert E. Lee, resplendent in his dress uniform, arrived first on his great horse Traveller. Lee entered Wilmer McLean's parlor with his aids and sat silently. His mind reeled about any options available to him except for surrender as he awaited Grant's arrival. Then a little over a half hour later, Grant with his aides and subordinate officers arrived; among them were General Phil Sheridan and George Armstrong Custer. Grant, dressed in a private's coat, entered the McLean house alone, while his staff respectfully waited outside in Wilmer's lawn.

The two men greeted each other. Then Grant began the conversation by saying "I met you once before, General Lee, while we were serving in Mexico, when you came over from General Scott's headquarters to visit Garland's brigade, to which I then belonged. I have always remembered your appearance, and I think I should have recognized you anywhere" (Davis, 1980).

"Yes," replied General Lee, "I know I met you on that occasion, and I have often thought of it and tried to recollect how you looked, but I have never been able to recall a single feature" (Ibid.).

Grant wrote out the surrender terms on a marble table in Wilmer's house. He told Lee that his officers could keep their side arms and their private horses. Lee asked if his cavalry troops could keep their horses, as each man owned them. Grant agreed. Lee's men of the Army of Northern Virginia had to take an oath of allegiance to the United States and then allowed to go home.

Grant walked down to the first step of the McLean home as Lee mounted Traveller. Quietly, Lee tipped his hat to Grant as he rode off to break the sad news to his army. As soon as both men had left the home, the Union soldiers began to pillage poor Wilmer's home. They emptied everything in the house that wasn't tied down. One of the souvenir hunters included George Armstrong Custer, who took the table upon which the surrender document had been signed.

Wilmer received just a handful of money for all of his trouble and personal belongings.

Wilmer McLean was unique in American History, in that the Civil War literally started in his front yard in Manassas, Virginia, and ended in the front parlor of the home he had moved to in the small village of Appomattox Court House.

After the war was over, Wilmer McLean moved his family back home to Manassas, Virginia.

Story Notes

The story of Wilmer McLean is well known to historians and natives of Appomattox Court House, Virginia. The stories of all the battles mentioned in this story can be found in the book, The Civil War *by Jeffery Ward and Ken Burns and the books written by the wonderful historian Burke Davis.*

I have been fortunate enough, in my lengthy career as a storyteller, to visit all the places mentioned in this story and have spent hours in conversation with National Park interpreters and with staff and management of countless museums and historic societies.

While in Charleston, South Carolina, I always make time to visit the South Carolina Historic Society. The city itself is a living museum, with many of the homes being over 300 years old. Battery Park is located where "the Cooper and Ashley Rivers come together to form the Atlantic Ocean." This is the site where the Confederate Army bombarded Fort Sumter. There is also a wonderful Naval Museum located at Patriot's Point that is open all year long.

Chapter 5

To Serve Proud and Free:
Isaiah Mays

Many military records from the Western campaigns of the 1860s through the 1880s are incomplete. That is unfortunate, because we have lost some important chapters in our country's history —and the stories of some of our greatest heroes. Such is the case for many of the Buffalo Soldiers who were recruited after the Civil War. Most were illiterate when they enlisted, but were not by the time of their discharge from the U.S. Army. Their births and deaths are recorded, but often the dates of enlistment and promotion are missing. In the following story, because of missing dates, certain dates in the life of Isaiah Mays are estimated, as noted in the story line.

It wasn't until May 29, 2009, that the story of Isaiah Mays finally made the newspaper. Even then, it wasn't a front-page feature. In fact, Isaiah Mays wasn't even alive— he'd been dead for 84 years! His story, though, began long before that, during his extraordinary life and military exploits that had somehow slipped through the pages of time and history for all of those years.

Slavery's Legacy

Isaiah Mays was born into slavery on February 16, 1858, in Carters Bridge, Virginia, near Leesburg. As a young child, he witnessed the end of the Civil War as, not fighting, but as witness to the thousands of veterans who made their way home. Six months after Lee's surrender, Isaiah and his family were freed along with all slaves by the ratification of the Thirteenth Amendment of the U.S. Constitution.

Unfortunately, being free wasn't really freedom for many of the South's African Americans. Abraham Lincoln did not live to see his Emancipation

Proclamation implemented. After Lincoln was assassinated, Vice President Andrew Johnson from Tennessee ascended to the presidency. Johnson had little desire to uphold the new rights of former slaves. His appointments of governors for the Southern states basically reinstituted their previous proslavery governments. Furthermore, the new legislatures enacted laws designed to keep African Americans in poverty and in servitude—making it all very legal. Ex-slaves who could not find work or had no steady employment could be arrested and ordered to pay stiff fines. If the prisoner could not pay the fine, they were hired out as virtual slaves. In many areas, children were forced to work as apprentices in local industries. This was, in fact, involuntary servitude, which had also been outlawed by the Constitution, but was never enforced because of President Johnson's social views and lack of political will.

Laws in Southern states prevented ex-slaves from purchasing land, and denied them decent wages for their work. It took another amendment to the Constitution to finally correct many of these illegal practices. That amendment was the Fourteenth Amendment, which guaranteed black men the right to vote. At that time, the former Confederate States were divided into military districts to enforce equality. Many of the ex-slaves were also veterans of the Union Army. One of the most famous regiments was the 54th Massachusetts Regiment that was the first all-black regiment of the Civil War and earned an undying glory for their assault on Fort Wagner, South Carolina, in 1863. Almost half of the regiment were killed, wounded, or captured. The survivors though, paved the way for the Union to recruit over 200,000 African Americans into the Army and Navy during the Civil War.

The Way West

When the Civil War ended, the United States rapidly expanded West; and the government looked to ways of getting soldiers out to the frontier. Many of the white soldiers, tired of four years of fighting, just wanted to go home and get on with their lives. In 1866, to overcome the shortage of manpower, Congress enacted legislation to create six all-African American regiments. These fighting men represented the nation's first all-black professional soldiers in a peacetime army, and among its ranks were many former slaves and Civil War veterans.

Sent West, the main objective of these soldiers was to protect the burgeoning frontier. It was also the first time many of Native Americans had ever seen a black man. The first African American to ever go West was York, William Clark's "man servant" on the Lewis and Clark expedition in 1804. There was also a mountain man who had traveled West shortly after York had. In 1824, young James Pierson Beckwourth began his sojourn into the Rocky Mountains. His father was his owner and gave his son emancipation papers before he left home, as black persons could not travel freely without them.

Young Beckwourth explored the Rocky Mountain West as few non-native men had in the past. The Crow Indians thought so much of him; he was made a war chief. Beckwourth, like other mountain men, married into friendly Native American tribes. And, like all mountain men, he knew how to spin a tall tale. Ironically, some of his true stories were so incredible that they sounded like lies. Since the sight of a "black-white man" was rare, Beckwourth took full advantage of it to obtain information about trapping and mountain passes. One such pass, now known as Beckwourth's Pass, is located in the Sierra Nevada mountain range in eastern California.

The story of this black explorer spread throughout the West, the East, and Europe. Thousands of people began their pilgrimage West after hearing about such adventures. One such youngster was Isaiah Mays. In his youth he'd witnessed the last days of fighting in Virginia and the return of a defeated Confederate Army. To escape the harsh reality of the inequities in the South and being forced to work for the old "planter families" that controlled the agriculture business, Isaiah Mays went North to join the U.S. Army.

Mays enlisted at Columbus Barracks in Columbus, Ohio. No date is recorded, but Isaiah was probably somewhere between 18 and 20 years old at that time. To Mays and thousands of other ex-slaves, the Army was a godsend. It paid $13.00 a month, provided a place to live, and also provided food and clothing. More than anything, the Army provided these men the opportunity to gain respect and to prove their right for equality. Isaiah was assigned to Company B of the 24th Infantry Regiment, one of the four-famed Buffalo Soldiers Regiments.

A Soldier's Life

The 24th Infantry Regiment was activated in 1869. It is likely that Mays was sent West to New Mexico and the Arizona Territory somewhere around 1875, during the Apache Wars.

No matter what uniform these soldiers wore, they could not escape the rampant racial discrimination that now also permeated the far Western frontiers. The discrimination came not only from the people they protected but also from white soldiers and officers. Many officers refused to be assigned to a black regiment. For example, when Lieutenant Colonel George Armstrong Custer was given a commission with the Buffalo Soldiers, he refused to accept it, emphatically saying he would take a lesser rank rather than command the 9th Cavalry.

His decision was rather fortuitous for the 9th, considering that Custer went on command the 7th Cavalry and was wiped out by the Lakota and Cheyenne on June 25, 1876, at the Little Big Horn River in Montana.

During the years 1866 through 1898, known as the "Indian Wars," some 10,000 Buffalo Soldiers served in the Western United States. The Cheyenne named them "Buffalo Soldiers" because of their short curly black hair, the color of their skin, and the tenacity and ferocity they displayed in battle.

Off the battlefield, these soldiers dealt with the hostility of the people they protected and racial discrimination from white officers and soldiers. Few in white America were ready for equality, even though since the founding of this country thousands of African Americans volunteered and died during the Revolutionary War, including one of the very first Americans killed, a freedman named Crispus Attucks in the 1770 Boston Massacre. Later, in 1778, the first black regiment in America's history, the First Rhode Island Regiment, defeated three major assaults by crack British troops in the Battle of Newport, Rhode Island. Out of the 180,000 who served in the Civil War, 33,000 died in defense of the Union.

Before joining the Army, Mays like most of the ex-slaves, was illiterate and had never been on a horse. These men not only learned how to ride, they also learned how to shoot quickly and accurately from atop of a running horse. The War Department required that every soldier be given a basic education, so they could read and write orders and documents. This excited Isaiah. It was another step closer to equality. The post schoolrooms were actually the fort's chapel. The fort's Chaplin acted as teacher and morale booster.

When not on patrol, Mays and his regiment constantly drilled. The Buffalo Soldiers were stationed from Oklahoma to Arizona and patrolled as far north as Wyoming and Montana. Their main duties were as escorts and guides; they protected miners, settlers, railroad workers, and mail carriers.

Army life is always harsh, especially for those in isolated areas. Mays and other Buffalo Soldiers may have complained about some things amongst themselves but never to anyone else. Humor was the constant when not on patrol. In the summer of 1888, the Western artist Fredric Remington accompanied a patrol of the 10th Regiment near Gila, Arizona. (This was no easy task for Remington, who at 5 feet 9 inches height weighed nearly 300 pounds.) He later chronicled his experience, "They occupied such time in joking and merriment as seemed fitted for growling. They may be tired and they may be hungry, but they do not see fit to augment their misery by finding fault with everybody and everything. In this particular they are charming men with whom to serve." (Remington, 1889)

Buffalo Soldiers from the 9th and 10th Regiments distinguished themselves all over the west and southwest including in Montana, Kansas, Colorado, Texas, and New Mexico including engagements against the Apaches, the Kiowa, the Comanche, and Lakota.

Isaiah Mays and the 24th Infantry patrolled south in Texas, New Mexico, and Arizona near the Mexican border. They also mapped over 35,000 square miles of West Texas and New Mexico and opened areas of this country never seen before by non-natives.

Mays had a bull neck, large arms, and a thick powerful chest. He stood somewhere between 5 feet 8 inches and 5 feet 10 inches tall. He and the others of his company were armed with Colt .45 revolver, a saber, and a 45.70 Springfield carbine rifle. Like other Buffalo Soldiers, he wore a flannel shirt, a dark blue blouse, with dark blue pants that were tucked in his over-the-knee boots.

No combat records of Isaiah Mays fighting the Apaches exists, but it is known that 5,000 U.S. Army troops relentlessly pursued the great Apache Geronimo all over New Mexico and Arizona, until he finally surrendered in 1886 in Skeleton Canyon on the New Mexico–Arizona border. After 25 years of successfully eluding the Army, Geronimo was the last Apache leader to finally surrender.

Ambushed

Two years later in June 1888, Isaiah Mays and his regiment moved to Fort Grant, Arizona Territory. Compared to Virginia's verdant countryside, the West's vast open landscapes left Mays awestruck. The East and North teamed with people, towns, and cities; but there were endless vistas of high desert, mountains, canyons, and sand that surrounded every part of his daily life. Mays, like the others, couldn't understand how anyone could live in the desert heat and survive the summer months. The country held a variety of scrub mesquite that tore both horse and human flesh with its thorns. The heat and the dust were unforgiving. Those who brought up the rear of any patrol had to wear neckerchiefs to prevent breathing in too much dust.

Life in the Army started with reveille at 5:45 a.m. and rarely ended with just 8 hours of work. Coffee, beans, and bacon were standard cuisine for breakfast. Hardtack and water were lunch while on patrol.

In addition to controlling the uneasy peace with the Apaches, the regiment built roads and went after illegal gun and whiskey traders who sought to sell their wares to the Indians. They tracked cattle rustlers and formed escorts for stagecoaches, and military paymasters.

On one such patrol, Corporal Isaiah Mays and 11 other men including Sergeant Benjamin Brown were ordered to escort a military payroll from Fort Grant to Fort Thomas. The Paymaster Joseph Wham rode in an army ambulance with a driver and clerk. Inside the ambulance, a strongbox held $28,345.10 (equivalent to a half million dollars today). These escorts were routine.

Near the small Mormon community of Pima, Arizona, in the narrow canyon Cottonwood Wash, over a dozen well-armed men ambushed the patrol. After a brave defense of the ambulance; and after Sergeant Brown and six others were wounded, Mays and the rest of the regiment were forced to take cover.

Sergeant Brown was shot five times and took a sixth bullet in his forearm, rendering his hand useless. Corporal Isaiah Mays then took command of the patrol and barked out orders to the other men as to where to go and where to fire. The highly fortified robbers, though, continued to pour down murderous fire from three sides on the soldiers below. Within the first shots of the ambush until 30 minutes later, all the men in the escort were seriously wounded. Near the end of the battle, Mays, though wounded in both legs, started out for help— walking and crawling.

Mays mostly crawled through desert sand, past mesquite, and over rocks; all the while avoiding rattlesnakes and desert lizards, including Gila monsters. After a few hours, Mays made his way to Cottonwood Ranch, where he got word out to the fort about the ambush and found assistance.

Miraculously Brown and Mays survived, though the wounds in Mays's legs crippled him. The robbers got away with the payroll, but seven of them were later identified and arrested. In the investigation that followed, eyewitness identifications were made by soldiers as well as the paymaster himself, and seven Mormon suspects from the Pima area were arrested.

Testimony given by the eyewitnesses was clear that none of the robbers wore masks or any kind of disguises, and the suspects were identified by name as well as description. Prejudice, though, overtook the evidence with the all-white jury, and all seven men were acquitted. This action was common in every-day life faced by the Buffalo Soldiers. The payroll of nearly $29,000 was never recovered.

Many Anglo-Americans questioned the mental and physical abilities of the Buffalo Soldiers. They were still perceived as inferior specimens of the human race, and their testimony wasn't taken seriously by white jurors (Ball, 2000).

Although Mays, Brown, and the others eventually recovered from their wounds, it is probable that Isaiah's leg wounds caused him trouble for the rest of his life. On February 15, 1890, both Corporal Isaiah Mays and Sergeant Benjamin Brown were awarded this nation's highest award for valor, the Medal of Honor, for duty "Above and Beyond the call of duty." At the time of his award, his superiors said, that Sergeant Brown and Corporal Mays were awarded the medal, "for gallantry and meritorious conduct." In the years between 1870 and 1890, 14 Buffalo Soldiers became recipients of the Medal of Honor. During their 30 years of service on the frontier, Buffalo Soldiers fought in nearly 200 battles.

Final Days

Isaiah Mays served in the Army for three more years; and in 1893, he finally was discharged. He never went back East. He remained in the Southwest, working as a laborer in New Mexico and Arizona until he could no longer work or was able to work. He finally applied for a pension from the U.S. Army that was then available to Medal of Honor recipients, for which he was denied. He appealed the government's ruling, and again was denied.

Because Isaiah Mays no longer had a means of making a living, and because he had no federal pension, the State of Arizona considered him "indigent." With no home or family to go to, State authorities committed 65-year-old, Medal of Honor recipient Isaiah Mays to the State Asylum for the Insane.

At the time, there was no legal process to incarcerate persons for reasons of "old age, tuberculosis, and feeble mindedness." By the time he was committed, the asylum held a population of close to 600 people. It was overcrowded and understaffed. Some of the patients were veterans of World War I (WWI) who were diagnosed as suffering from "acute melancholia." The military called it "shell shock." Today it is called "posttraumatic stress disorder."

For this valiant soldier, who just 20 years before, fulfilled his wish to serve proud and free, life in this institution must have truly been "hell on earth." After three years of living in this environment, Corporal Isaiah Mays passed away in 1925. The State's and this country's betrayal of Isaiah Mays continued after his death. State officials unceremoniously wrapped him in a sheet and buried him in a pauper's grave at the All Souls Cemetery.

Isaiah Mays's Final Resting Place

For almost 80 years, a modest brick-like marker with a number etched on it was the only gravesite marker for Isaiah Mays. In 1935, records of his exact burial place were destroyed in a hospital fire, along with those of all other cemetery interments. Had it not been for dedicated hospital staff of the new Arizona State Hospital and a veterans' group called "The Missing in America Project," Isaiah Mays would have remained forgotten, instead of receiving tribute as a recipient of this nation's highest military award for valor.

The sole purpose of The Missing in America Project is to locate, identify and inter the unclaimed remains of American Veterans through joint efforts of private, state and federal organizations. The group also provides honor and respect to those who have served this country by securing a final resting place for these forgotten heroes (The Missing in America Project).

Isaiah's grave was finally located in what was an isolated trash-filled, weed-infested vacant lot in downtown Phoenix. In 2001, the lot was cleaned up, and the U.S. Department of Veterans Affairs authorized a Medal of Honor headstone to be placed on his gravesite.

A few years later, The Missing in America Project in conjunction with the Buffalo Soldiers Motorcycle Club of Phoenix and the Old Guard Riders, a motorcycle escort service, sought to change Isaiah Mays's final resting place.

Representatives from these organizations petitioned Maricopa County Superior Court to exhume Corporal Mays's remains from his interment place. On March 5, 2009, the Superior Court Judge issued a court order authorizing exhumation of the remains of Corporal Isaiah Mays from the property of the

Arizona State Hospital by the Old Guard Riders and The Missing in America Project.

The court order was delivered to the hospital director and a copy was faxed to Arlington National Cemetery. Arlington officials responded and forwarded an internment schedule for Isaiah Mays.

Isaiah's remains were exhumed and cremated. The urn holding his ashes was engraved in a manner befitting a Medal of Honor recipient.

Thus, on the morning of May 21, 2009, Corporal Isaiah Mays began his journey back to his native Virginia. This time, he was going to a resting place for America's heroes, Arlington National Cemetery. The Old Guard Rider Funeral Escort Team, members of the Arizona Buffalo Soldiers Motorcycle Club, and other riders escorted him. As the escort crossed the United States, more riders joined until they finally reached Arlington.

On Memorial Day, Friday, May 29, 2009, at 3:00 p.m., the former slave from Virginia was buried as a national hero in Arlington National Cemetery, where he can now be remembered as one who served his country, proud and free.

Story Notes

I first heard the story of Corporal Isaiah Mays from my friend Colonel Ward Nickisch near the Vietnam Veteran's Memorial at Angel Fire, New Mexico. Researching this story was difficult but became a labor of love because Isaiah Mays had become a forgotten hero. I felt strongly about including his story, because our veterans came from every walk of life and asked nothing except to serve and honor their country. This recognition seems the least we can offer.

The geographic descriptions are based on my own visits to the areas in this story. I have performed and traveled in Leesburg, Virginia, as well as throughout Arizona and New Mexico. The physical description of Isaiah Mays comes from the only known photograph taken of him.

The historic information I have gleaned comes from Arlington National Cemetery's official website, and other sources (listed later).

Chapter 6

To Walk Softly and Carry a Big Stick: Theodore Roosevelt

"Do what you can, with what you have, where you are." Theodore Roosevelt advised. These words echoed then and now in many a veteran's heart as they brave the battlefield and as they help to protect America.

In April 1897, Theodore Roosevelt was appointed assistant secretary of the Navy under President William McKinley.

A year later, on February 5, 1898, the battleship USS *Maine* exploded in Havana Harbor. Not sure why this explosion happened, over 260 sailors were killed. Theodore Roosevelt instantly realized that involvement in the Spanish American War was inevitable. Unlike Roosevelt, President McKinley was reluctant to participate in the war because he had seen war firsthand, the American Civil War.

On February 25, that same year, secretary of the Navy, John D. Long, began his vacation from work, directing Roosevelt, who was to fill in for him, not to "take any such step affecting the policy of the Administration without consulting with the President or myself . . . my intention was to have you look after the routine of the office . . ." Long continued, saying he was ". . . anxious to have no unnecessary occasion for a sensation in the papers" (Jeffers, 1996).

In spite of Long's warnings, Roosevelt took advantage of his absence and began preparing for war by ordering the navy fleets to ready themselves at a moment's notice. He further requested Congress to begin enlisting men, approved buying auxiliary cruisers, and much more. He then telegrammed the Navy Admiral George Dewey to prepare for war. Long was extremely disturbed and enraged at Roosevelt's actions. He didn't cancel Roosevelt's orders but resolved never to permit the zealous Roosevelt to be in charge again.

Theodore Roosevelt had made it clear in the past that if war erupted, he personally wished to give up his desk position for an assignment at the frontlines;

and he worked to improve his odds of fighting on the front. He shot a letter to New York Congressman William Astor Chandler and his young army surgeon friend Leonard Wood letting them know of his intent to be on the frontlines, just in case they might be planning to form a regiment.

President McKinley was determined to avoid war. But Roosevelt, at a cabinet meeting, vehemently expressed his views to the president, telling him that war "was compatible with our national honor, or with the claims of humanity on behalf of the wretched women and children of Cuba" (Ibid.). The Congress and newspapers supported war as well. Thus, on April 20, President McKinley finally relinquished and with Congress on his side, he informed the Spanish government they had three days to free Cuba to prevent war. McKinley began his request to call for 125,000 volunteers.

Russell Alger, secretary of war, knew Roosevelt's desire to fight and offered him his own regiment. But Roosevelt, knowing he wasn't capable of such a command, suggested his friend Leonard Wood be the one in charge. Roosevelt, further suggested to Alger the he be assigned the rank of lieutenant colonel instead.

The unit, nicknamed "Rough Riders" was comprised of a strange but impressive group of athletes, cowboys, and frontiersmen, as well as sons of some prominent citizens. As the call went out, more men lined up to apply.

As early as the next day, Roosevelt, along with Colonel Wood and their men, left to fight against the Spanish troops at Las Guasimas. While resting to meet up with General Young and his troops, Roosevelt and Wood's men were soon ambushed. The Rough Riders tried firing back but were initially baffled as to where the Spanish infantry's shots were coming from. What they soon discovered was that the infantry was using smokeless powder. Once they figured out their positions, the Rough Riders aggressively shot at the Spanish causing them to flee. One bullet narrowly missed Roosevelt's head, and hit a tree, which shielded him but also sprayed splinters and dust into his face and eyes.

Fighting the Spaniards was challenging, but the battle promoted Colonel Wood to brigade commander. That meant Roosevelt was elevated to colonel of the Rough Riders.

Kettle Hill and San Juan Hill

In the stifling Cuban heat came the orders: the Rough Riders were to advance up Kettle Hill. With regular troops attacking the hill from a different side, Roosevelt, on his horse Texas, appealed to his men to push forward. Through continued advancement, Roosevelt found he was leading the entire attack! Those watching the maneuver felt the Rough Riders didn't stand a chance against the well-armed Spaniards.

Roosevelt continued his ride to within 40 yards from the hill's summit only to be stopped by a wire fence. Dismounting his horse Texas and being outpaced by the orderly Henry Bradshar, and along with other Rough Riders, they soon reached the summit. Shortly thereafter, rifle and cannon fire began raining down on them and they retreated into the Spanish trenches and behind a sugar kettle. It was this sugar kettle that the hill received its name Kettle Hill from.

Roosevelt and his men continued their steady charge of fire until they penetrated the Spanish line. Between the combined efforts of the other advancing troops and Roosevelt's men, they pushed back the Spanish forces. After Roosevelt ordered another charge, the Spaniards retreated to the nearby San Juan Hill. Unbeknownst to Roosevelt only five soldiers had followed him; three of them were immediately wounded. While the remaining two men held the ground, Roosevelt made his way through enemy fire to the main line where he confronted his men for abandoning him. He quickly learned the troops hadn't heard the order; nor had they seen Roosevelt facing enemy troops with only five men. Roosevelt ordered his men to charge again and they all followed. The Spanish were soon defeated and the Americans tenuously held Kettle and San Juan Hills. Of its 490 men, Rough Riders lost 89.

Many of the war experts agreed that Roosevelt's leadership and fighting spirit were the strongest factors leading to eventual surrender by the Spaniards on July 17.

By the end of the war, the 10th Cavalry military unit received five Medals of Honor and 26 Certificates of Merit. Theodore Roosevelt felt his 10th Cavalry were "... brave men worthy of respect, I don't think any Rough Rider will ever forget the tie that binds us to the Tenth cavalry" (Jeffers, 1996).

Upon returning home, Roosevelt heard someone shouting from the crowds asking him how he felt about the war. Roosevelt replied back, "I've had a bully time and a bully fight. I feel as big and as strong as a Bull Moose!" (Ibid.). Roosevelt now held the role of being one of the most famous Americans. The legend of his leadership had been born. In 1898, he rode the wave of popularity into the governorship of New York.

In 1900, Theodore Roosevelt became vice president, serving under William McKinley. When the president was assassinated in September 1901, he was thrust into the presidency, thus, becoming the 26th president of the United States. He was elected in 1904 to another term.

Immediately following the Spanish American War, some officers suggested Theodore Roosevelt be awarded the Medal of Honor. Secretary of War Alger thought differently. Alger's anger toward Roosevelt for his influencing Congress to support the war was never forgiven. So Alger refused to endorse the recommendation. Without his support, all efforts to award the medal to Roosevelt failed. This proved to be a great disappointment to Roosevelt.

However, in January 2001, President William Clinton finally bestowed the Medal of Honor on Theodore Roosevelt, more than 80 years after Roosevelt's death. This was the first time in history that both father and son were posthumously awarded the Medal of Honor. Theodore Roosevelt's award stated:

LIEUTENANT COLONEL THEODORE ROOSEVELT
UNITED STATES ARMY

For conspicuous gallantry and intrepidity at the risk of his life above and beyond the call of duty:

Lieutenant Colonel Theodore Roosevelt distinguished himself by acts of bravery on 1 July, 1898, near Santiago de Cuba, Republic of Cuba, while leading a daring charge up San Juan Hill. Lieutenant Colonel Roosevelt, in total disregard for his personal safety, and accompanied by only four or five men, led a desperate and gallant charge up San Juan Hill, encouraging his troops to continue the assault through withering enemy fire over open countryside. Facing the enemy's heavy fire, he displayed extraordinary bravery throughout the charge, and was a sick to reach the enemy trenches, where he quickly killed one of the enemy with his pistol, allowing his men to continue the assault. His leadership and valor turned the tide in the Battle for San Juan Hill. Lieutenant Colonel Roosevelt's extraordinary heroism and devotion to duty are in keeping with the highest traditions of military service and reflect great credit upon himself, his unit, and the United States Army. (Congressional Medal of Honor Society, 1898)

Story Notes

I've have always been enthralled with the history and stories about Theodore Roosevelt, even more so after interviewing Ray Bauml (Chapter 14) and hearing of his many exploits during WWII. Ray stole Theodore Roosevelt's son's jeep on a joy ride. It gave me a more personal side of president Roosevelt.

Chapter 7

To Vanish in the Morning: Blanche Hennebery and George MacCrae

This is a little-known story of an incident that happened in Nova Scotia, Canada, during WWI. It's called the Halifax Disaster. Twenty-four years later, one of the victims in this story became an elite World War II (WWII) marine.

As in all wars, some of the greatest tragedies are not caused by combat, but by humanity's inability to act when faced with impending disaster. Such was the case in Halifax, Nova Scotia, in 1917—a casualty of war not caused by combat or battle, but one that dwarfed those casualties in the destruction it wrought.

Canada's entrance into WWI was automatic after Great Britain entered it in 1914. But the country was ill prepared for war. At the time there were only 3,110 men in Canada's standing army, and they possessed only a fledgling navy. However, within weeks of recruiting, over 32,000 men had volunteered and gathered for military training. Their small navy also began to grow. Within two years, Halifax became the Canadian Navy's main base, and the most important army garrison in the country.

Hundreds of military ships, troop transports, and supply ships now filled the great harbor and waterways. These ships regularly cruised between Nova Scotia and England bringing in the much-needed ammunition and supplies for allied troops. French and Belgium ships were also common sights on Canadian shores.

All of their trips were hazardous. Even if the ships survived the North Atlantic's seas and weather, they were constantly under attack by German U-boats (submarines). Submarine warfare was a new development in the annals of maritime history, and it was initially looked upon by the English and Germans with disdain. It wasn't until Germany faced economic disaster that they turned to submarine warfare.

At the time, England ruled the seas, and thus had slowly squeezed the life-blood of Germany's war effort through her naval superiority. With the coming of the U-boat, Germany began devastating many of the ships crossing the Atlantic. Fortunately, for the allied ships, German torpedoes were not very accurate and many were duds. They didn't explode on impact. So the Germans tried a new tactic.

The Germans used giant mine-laying submarines. These ships were capable of trans-Atlantic crossings; and they laid down explosive mines in the shipping lanes. With this new approach, more than one ship went to a watery grave.

Then, on December 6, 1917, in Halifax, Nova Scotia, Canada experienced the worst loss of life in its history.

It was on this day that the French ship *Mont Blanc* collided with the Belgian ship *Imo* in the narrows between northern Halifax and the southern end of the City of Dartmouth.

The *Imo* left Halifax harbor on its way to New York at the same time as a French munitions ship, the *Mont Blanc*, was headed for a rendezvous with a convoy. When the two ships collided, there initially appeared to be no serious damage to either ship. But then a fire broke out on the *Mont Blanc*.

Fire aboard a ship is always dangerous for the crew, but in this case, it was disastrous. The *Mont Blanc* was laden with over a million pounds of trinitrotoluene (TNT), picric acid, and gun cotton. Benzol, which is extremely flammable, was on the top deck, and it spilled in the collision and began burning furiously. The captain and crew did their best to extinguish the blaze, but soon realized it was impossible. If they were to survive, they had to abandon ship.

Crowds gathered at Halifax Harbor, watching the spark-filled smoke billowing from the crippled ship. Crews of nearby ships quickly headed toward the *Mont Blanc* to douse the blaze. But the ship's captain and crew were frantically rowing in the opposite direction toward Dartmouth shore, yelling at the onlookers to run.

Just then the *Mont Blanc* rammed Pier 6, setting it ablaze.

On shore, even more onlookers gathered to see the fire. Some came to watch the *Mont Blanc* burn. Others thought she would sink.

Instead, at exactly 9:04 a.m., the *Mont Blanc* exploded.

The devastating blast tore through that cold clear morning; and like the ship herself, people, buildings, and houses vanished, as did half of Halifax and the City of Dartmouth.

Denver, Colorado, resident Suzanne Sigona recalls a story her grandmother told her about that December day.

Grandmother [Blanche Henneberry], only 5 years old, was on her way to school with her brother just blocks from the harbor when the

Mont Blanc exploded. She quietly spoke of surviving the blast, and the horror of grabbing her brother to protect him, when his arm came off in her hand. It was a miracle that either of them survived. Grandmother's five other siblings did not.

Grandmother . . . was in the emergency evacuation area which I later learned was the YMCA. A nun came in with her father, Benjamin Henneberry. He looked at the children and announced to the nun that his daughter was not there.

There were tears in my eyes as grandmother calmly continued her story. She explained that she was in the room crying when the nun returned and asked what was wrong.

Grandmother cried, 'That's my father and he doesn't want me anymore.

The nun quickly left to find Blanch's father and then explained to him why she was unrecognizable; she was covered with burns, soot and cinders. The same cinders that left the permanent tattooing of her face.

(Sigona, 1994)

Three-month-old George MacCrae was cradled in his grandmother's arms at the moment of the *Mount Blanc*'s explosion. She was standing in front of the fireplace in their home. George's father was a colonel in the Canadian Army. Fortunately, for the MacCraes, their home was much farther inland than was the Henneberry home when the ship exploded. While his grandmother held him, a piece of glass, "the size of a man's hand" flew from the windowpane and struck young George in the face. Miraculously, it was the flat of the glass that hit him. Had it been the edge, it would have decapitated him. The concussion of the blast buckled the large stone hearth in front of the fireplace. George's grandmother, while holding him leaned back into the hearth to keep it from falling on them. Fortunately, she wasn't alone; George's father was there, and he too held the hearth in place.

The devastation of the *Mont Blanc*'s explosion flattened everything within 2,600 feet and damaged everything within a 1-mile radius of the water. The explosion was heard from 300 miles away from Prince Edward Island to the north to the state of Maine to the south.

Eyewitnesses reported that the water around the *Mont Blanc* vaporized and the streets of Halifax and Dartmouth were flooded as a huge pressure wave poured into the cities. This manmade tsunami rocked ships in the nearby narrow and caused some of them to break their moorings. The wave also swept many of the onlookers into the harbor, where they drowned. This gigantic wave traveled north across over to Dartmouth and into Native American settlement of Micmac. Then it vanished.

Flying glass from shattered windows tore through many of those watching the disaster unfold from the relative safety from a high vantage point from the narrows. Scores of people were blinded.

As if the explosion and the wave weren't bad enough, they were followed by fires. Cinders from the explosion billowed with the smoke and burning debris as well as burning embers from the fire at Pier 6. It all spread into city buildings and ignited many of the wooden structures including business and homes. Other fires broke out as wood stoves toppled over in homes from the shock of the blast.

Shrapnel created from the ship's body ripped through people, horses, and structures throughout both cities, and rained down on everything in the blast zone. Some 1,900 people were killed and more than 9,000 were injured. About 1,600 buildings were destroyed. Another 12,000 homes were severely damaged. Close to 6,000 people were left homeless while another 25,000 were left with inadequate housing. The blast from the *Mont Blanc* was the most powerful man-made explosion in history until the atomic bomb blast of Hiroshima and Nagasaki almost 30 years later.

Rescue workers had more than they could handle. Luckily the telegraph lines and some of the telephone lines were operating, all sending urgent calls for help.

And, fortunately, the army and navy personnel stationed in Halifax readily gave the cities "disciplined and organized" relief workers. They mobilized immediately, and prevented another potential disaster as the ammunition magazine caught fire. Acting quickly, the military men pumped thousands of gallons of water on it and then dumped the munitions in the harbor to prevent anything from setting it off.

As word of the disaster spread, massive rescue efforts mobilized throughout Nova Scotia, Quebec Province—even as far away as New Zealand. The greatest aid effort though came from the City of Boston, Massachusetts. Boston was the largest and closest seaport that could take immediate and comprehensive relief aid. In addition to sending doctors, nurses, and medical supplies, Boston sent food, clothing, and transportation equipment. Although not realized immediately, the only access to Halifax would be from the sea.

Rumors ran rampant throughout the city. There were many people who believed that the *Mont Blanc*'s explosion was caused by German sabotage. Others felt that bombs dropped from a large German Zeppelin triggered the day's events. Panicked people began taking their frustrations and anger out on their own citizens. People with German sounding names were beaten without any cause other than the sound of their name.

Then, to make things worse, the next day the weather changed. A cold breeze filled the air. Though winter was officially two weeks away, this late autumn day felt as though the city was in the dead of winter.

Local barometers began falling, and later that night, so did the snow. And the snow didn't stop. The breeze picked up into 50-mile-an-hour winds; and snow piled up. The blizzard that hit Halifax and Dartmouth on December 7 and the next two days stymied all rescue operations. The horror it created seared through the psyche of even battle-hardened veterans who were there. They found bodies that were burned beyond belief. Many of the dead could not be recognized. Total families were wiped out.

Some people, trapped in the ruins of the buildings, froze to death and were covered in their house's rubble as well as the accumulating snows. All aid coming from trains and any other overland routes was halted because of the weather. Trains trying to bring relief workers in as well as those transporting the injured out could not plow through the sheer volumes of snow that covered the tracks. Many of the injured died.

The storm—the worst blizzard to hit Halifax in over 30 years—forced rescuers to abandon searching wrecked homes, and it delayed the burial of the dead.

Finally, within days, the fires were brought under control; however, between the explosion, the tidal wave, the fire, and blizzard, over 20,000 people beyond the dead and injured were left totally destitute.

Survivors' Tales

Young George MacCrae and his family miraculously survived all of the disasters that took place in December and eventually moved to the United States. Twenty-five years later, George joined the U.S. Marine Corps to become an elite Marine Raider. He served in the Pacific theater in some of the bloodiest fighting of WWII. George MacCrae not only survived the greatest war the world has ever known, but, as a toddler, he had survived the greatest disaster in Canada's history.

Suzanne Sigona has never had the opportunity to visit her grandmother's home of Halifax, Nova Scotia, but hopes to make the journey on December 6 of any year.

Each year since that time, the City of Halifax commemorates the anniversary with the ringing of 14 bells at the exact time of the tragedy.

> I have not visited my grandmother's grave since she was buried over twenty years ago, but I keep her spirit close to me each day. One day I will go to Halifax on December 6th and listen to the bells chime at exactly four minutes past 9:00 a.m., to celebrate her life, and to remember those who came before me. (Sigona, 1994)

The people of Halifax and Dartmouth have also never forgotten, not only the tragedy and devastation of that October day but also the incredible kindness of those who brought life giving aid and hope by sea. Every year the people of Halifax present the City of Boston, Massachusetts, with a towering Christmas tree to express their gratitude for the help they sent in December 1917.

———————————

Story Notes

I met Suzanna Sigona in 1994 at the Vietnam Veterans Memorial and again at the Wall in Washington, D.C. She had started volunteering at the Memorial in 1988, and was told then she needed to meet me and share her grandmother's story. Her story is linked to what is called posttraumatic stress, which her grandmother suffered as a result of the Mont Blanc *ramming the pier in Halifax. As told to me by Suzanne, Blanche learned to carry her grief and resume her life. She never spoke of the explosion again.*

Chapter 8

We Laid Aside the Citizen: Joe Angelo and the Veterans' Bonus March

It is reported that George Washington once said, "When We Assumed the Soldier, We did not Lay Aside the Citizen." If correct, this next story documents that the most egregious act of "laying aside the citizen" occurred when the U.S. Army made their last mounted cavalry charge against its own veterans!

Until 1916, Joe Angelo lived an ordinary, quiet life in Camden, New Jersey. But that year, like almost everyone else in the country, Joe knew that the war was either coming to America or the country was going to the war in Europe or Mexico. In May 1915, the *Lusitania* had been sunk. Now, just 10 months later, the United States woke up to the news that Mexican revolutionaries, under the command of the infamous Francisco "Pancho" Villa had invaded the sleepy border town of Columbus, New Mexico.

For years, the Mexican Revolution had raged to the south; and most Americans, including those who lived in border towns, never felt threatened by it. In Columbus, the feeling of safety was underlined by the fact that there was a detachment of 350 U.S. soldiers from the 13th Cavalry stationed at Camp Furlong on the outskirts of town. The camp was located between the town and the Mexican border.

But in the early morning hours of March 9, 1916, the town and its security changed forever. Along with about 500–600 revolutionaries, Villa crossed the border, simultaneously attacking the town and the army camp, and catching everyone by surprise.

Fortunately, Villa's men concerned themselves with the pillaging and burning of the business district rather than killing civilians. What puzzled many in the aftermath was that Villa's men didn't do more damage to Camp Furlong.

Many Columbus residents were awakened by the gunfire; and they fled into the desert or found refuge in the schoolhouse and the Hoover Hotel.

With the first sounds of gunfire, Camp Furlong officers and soldiers quickly set up 30-caliber machine guns in front of the hotel and on East Boundary Street, producing a murderous cross fire for anyone caught in the middle. The raid lasted for about an hour and a half. Villa lost around 75 men; and during the attack on Columbus, 18 Americans died. Most were civilians.

The U.S. Army, under the command of General John J. Pershing, was ordered to pursue Pancho Villa until he was caught or killed. Pershing and his men spent a year in pursuit without results before being recalled to make preparations to go to Europe.

In 1917, Joe Angelo, like millions of other American men, did what he was asked to do; he signed up to go to war in France and Belgium. He volunteered and ended up in the Meuse-Argonne with the 1st Brigade Tank Corps. Joe was an enlisted aid to one of the captains of the brigade. On September 16, 1918, during a battle near Cheppy, France, Joe's company came under heavy machine gun fire. During the fighting, his captain was wounded in the leg and buttocks, and couldn't walk or run to get out of the line of fire.

Joe, who was not a big man, crawled over to his wounded captain; then, making his way through enemy fire, he carried the man to a shell hole. He put the captain in the hole for cover from enemy fire, and remained with him, leaving the captain only twice to run through the murderous fire to carry orders to passing tanks. Hours later, reinforcement arrived and extricated Joe and his captain. For his action, Joe Angelo received the Distinguished Service Cross, the Army's highest award for valor. Little did Joe realize he would cross the path of his captain, George S. Patton, in the future.

So, Joe Angelo had become a hero; when the war ended in November, he, like every other man who served, returned home forever. He tried to settle down in his home of Camden, but home life in the United States had changed too. For one thing, the sale of alcohol had been banned.

There was a very popular song at the end of WWI that asked the question "How you gonna keep 'em down on the farm after they've seen Paree?" It was very appropriate, particularly if one of those veterans wanted a drink of liquor.

For years, the Women's Christian Temperance Union and many other organizations sought to ban alcohol. They believed a ban defended the population from the bad behaviors of alcohol abuse. So, in 1919, after years of trying, the Eighteenth Amendment to the Constitution was amended and on January 16, 1920, the sale of alcohol became illegal.

It was a big change but not as big as the change that followed. Women won a huge victory in the law of the land when in August of that same year the Nineteenth Amendment to the Constitution gave women of the United States the right to vote! That fight was another conflict that had deeply divided this country. As a matter of fact, the final vote to ratify the amendment came down to one person, Harry Burn. Harry, a 24-year-old legislator from Tennessee, opposed the Women's Suffrage Movement. But when time came for him to cast his deciding vote, it was a woman who convinced him to change his mind. That woman was his mother.

The Victorian era in the United States didn't quietly exit off stage. It was violently pushed off, as the Roaring Twenties danced its way into history with jazz and illegal liquor. Women's hairstyles and hemlines became shorter; and for nine years most of America partied.

The sale of alcohol was now illegal, but the Prohibition ultimately produced the opposite effect that the temperance movement wanted. The direct cause of organized crime in this country was the immense profits that could be made by selling illegal liquor. Underground drinking clubs called "speakeasies" were numerous throughout America, especially in New York, Chicago, and other large cities. Massive quantities of liquor were smuggled in from Canada overland and via the Great Lakes.

The rise of violent crime shocked America's conscience, as gangsters like Al Capone and "Bugs" Moran sought to kill each other off without regard to innocent bystanders. That violence reached a crescendo when Capone had his men slaughter seven people in a Chicago garage on February 14, 1927, in an act that became known in history as the "St. Valentine's Day Massacre."

Radio came of age, as did the recording industry. Motion pictures soon changed the world of entertainment that same year with the advent of the first movie that had sound. This "talky" was the *Jazz Singer* featuring one of this country's most popular singing stars Al Jolson.

Then in October 1929, it all came crashing down. Banks all over the United States failed because of Wall Street's investments. Thus began the Great Depression.

The Depression's great wake savaged the savings of millions of Americans. People were forced from their homes. Soup lines became commonplace in all of the major cities. To make matters worse, drought ravaged America's heartland. In Oklahoma and parts of Texas the land was parched from lack of rain, overplowing, and overgrazing. The wind came up, and the sand and dust began to blow. These dust storms wreaked havoc in the Midwest, which became known as the "dust bowl." The area had already been hit with 14 "black blizzards" and there were predictions of many more to come. This disaster prompted a new migration to California's promised lands on wagon and automobile trails. What followed for the next 10 years was the worst depression this country had ever known.

And tens of thousands of its victims were WWI veterans. Joe Angelo saw what was happening in the country he had fought for, and it saddened him.

* * *

In March 1932, a few hundred WWI veterans had commandeered a train in Oregon, and made their way to Washington, D.C., to ask the Congress and the president for payment of a promised bonus to cope with the economic downfall of the country. When the train reached Council Bluffs, Iowa, they found other veterans had the same idea. The few hundred now became thousands, and more came from all directions, heading to Washington, D.C., in support of Representative Wright Patman's bill which asked for early payment of their bonus.

In 1924, the Congress had voted to give these veterans $2.4 billion but over a 20-year period, so as to not put a strain on its fund. As of 1932, these veterans had not received any payment. The veterans now demanded passage of a bill providing immediate payment.

The veterans called themselves the Bonus Expeditionary Force. They camped out in a variety of building and places provided by the Washington, D.C., police department. These veterans conducted themselves in a peaceful way. But when the bill was defeated in Congress, in June, the veterans were given no other choice than to leave Washington. They refused. They said that they would camp out in the shantytown they'd established dubbed "Hooverville" (named after President Hoover, who was widely blamed for the country's economic woes) until the Congress changed their minds.

They had come in an orderly way and would stay orderly; but they chose to exercise their constitutional rights of free speech and demonstration.

Chief of Police Pelham Glassford was himself a veteran. His heart went out to these brothers in uniform. The organizers of the march told the police, there was to be no violence, "no panhandling, no drinking, and no radicalism." The utmost courtesy was extended to all. In fact, these veterans had no place to go. Many had their families with them.

By late July, the temperature and tempers began to heat up. The hot humid air of mid-summer in Washington, D.C., made life in Hooverville almost unbearable. The area's local citizens stepped in and helped keep the lid on what was about to boil over. They helped feed and clothe those veterans who were suffering the most. And no one turned food away, especially to the veterans' wives and children.

But on July 28, 1932, a bonus of $528 became payable to the family of William Huska, one of the veterans, when he was shot to death by a Washington, D.C., police officer. The policeman who killed him panicked when the huge crowd of WWI veterans confronted him and the other police officers in the nation's capital. That one gunshot touched off the greatest civil disturbance in the history of the nation's capital.

Within seconds of Huska's death, the other veterans who gathered there began throwing rocks, bricks, and other objects at the police. The police responded with tear gas and riot clubs. As the situation worsened, President Herbert Hoover took action by ordering the U.S. Army to put down what he felt was an insurrection.

Hoover's chief of staff, General Douglas MacArthur, was ordered to evict the veterans only to clear Pennsylvania Ave. MacArthur ignored the limits of this order. (It would not be the last time this flamboyant man would disobey a direct order from a president.)

On July 28, 1932, General MacArthur ordered a mounted U.S. Cavalry charge. He directed his Chief of Staff Major Dwight D. Eisenhower to carry out this action. Eisenhower then ordered four troops of cavalry, commanded by Major George S. Patton to follow through with their orders. With drawn sabers and fixed bayonets, Patton's men charged into the throng of American veterans. Tanks were brought in; and MacArthur had the veteran's camps burned. Two panicked policemen shot two of the veterans dead. Tear gas was launched into the shacks built by the veterans and their families. An infant died of asphyxiation. By nightfall, bayonets, sabers, and gas had injured hundreds of veterans. Throughout his career Patton often said, "May God have mercy on my enemies, because I won't" (Patton, official website). Mercy, it seems, was in short supply on July 28, 1932.

MacArthur ignored President Hoover's order to not to pursue the Bonus Marchers across the Anacostia River to their main encampment. He commanded his men across the bridge anyway. Then they torched the main encampment. The blaze could be seen for miles. Women and children, blinded from the tears in their eyes, frantically ran from their dwellings without gathering their meager belongings. When seven-year-old Eugene King turned back to his tent to get his pet rabbit, a soldier yelled at him to leave and, without provocation, bayoneted him through the leg.

Joe Angelo watched as one self-confident cavalry officer led his soldiers with drawn bayonets against his Anacostia shack, he suddenly recognized a man he'd known from his WWI experiences in France—George S. Patton. But Joe, too, fled for his life from his Anacostia dwelling.

Later MacArthur justified his attack on former members of the U.S. Army by claiming that the Bonus March was part of a "communist revolution" taking place in America. Ironically, this incident was the last mounted charge in the history of the U.S. Cavalry. And it was perpetrated against its own veterans.

One of the so-called "communists" was Joe Angelo. Days before, he had come down from New Jersey, broke and hungry like all of these veterans of the Great War. Joe survived the fighting, and after the violence was over, he requested an audience with Major George S. Patton. Patton denied knowing Angelo. He refused to see Joe and told his aids, "I do not know this man. Take him away and under no circumstances allow him to return. If he approaches me again, shoot him" (Zezima, 2005).

You see, Patton was the captain whose life Joe Angelo had saved during the battle near Cheppy, France, in September 1918.

The next day, the *New York Times* ran an article under the headline: "A Calvary Major Evicts Veteran Who Saved His Life in Battle."

Angelo never forgave Patton; and the two men never saw each other again. But years later, Patton described his participation against the Bonus Marchers as one of the most shameful events in his own life.

This incident, in the summer of 1932, horrified the nation. How could the president of the United States order this kind of violence against the nation's heroes?

Fourteen years earlier these same men had been praised with songs and parades. Entertainers traveled all over the United States to military camps to perform for these men about to be sent to war. The great sharp shooter Annie Oakley, who was now 58 years old, would come out and still not miss a target in her demonstrations and would tell stories of her days in Buffalo Bill's Wild West Show. She particularly retold the tale of her traveling in Germany 20 years earlier and putting on one of her most famous shots of shooting a lit cigarette out of the mouth of her husband. She related a story about how during a tour of Germany in 1894, Kaiser Wilhelm was so impressed with that shot that he wanted Annie to shoot one out of his mouth. Not wanting to take any chances with a Crown Head's safety, she agreed to shoot the cigarette out of his hand instead.

And now with America at war with Germany, Annie Oakley reportedly joked that had she known that he'd start the war, she would have purposely missed while trying to shoot the cigarette out of his mouth. The crowds always roared with laughter over that story, and were awed that she could still make that shot. These shows and demonstrations inspired troops to do much better on the rifle range.

Annie Oakley didn't live to see what had happened to some of those same veterans in the summer of 1932. If she had, she too would likely have been horrified.

And what about President Hoover? Did he live to regret his decision?

Unfortunately for Herbert Hoover, 1932 was also an election year. His actions in July culminated his four years of having been in office during the Great Depression. He was thrown out of office in his reelection bid by one of the greatest electoral landslides in American history. The new president, Franklin Delano Roosevelt, took office in the winter of 1933 with a promise of a new tomorrow and a "New Deal."

Of course, there was no immediate New Deal for these veterans. Roosevelt also refused to pay out the bonus; although three years later, in 1935, he did send hundreds of these veterans to Florida to work on the overseas railroad. On the Labor Day weekend of that year, the strongest recorded hurricane in history came roaring through Upper Matacombe Key and killed 259 of these veterans. The 200 plus mile per hour winds acted as a gigantic sand blaster that literally tore flesh away from many of the victims' bodies. Others were washed out to sea. To add to the indignity of what these men endured during the war, their bodies were cremated en masse.

The irony of this story is that Matacombe is a mispronunciation of two Spanish words *"Mata Hombre"* that translates into "to kill man."

Joe Angelo went back to New Jersey and endured another eight years of the Depression until WWII broke out in December 1941. Many of the veterans who served in WWI and survived the Bonus March never forgot their love of this country and volunteered for service again after the Japanese attacked Pearl Harbor on December 7, 1941. At age 53, Joe Angelo was too old to enter the service again. He, like many others of that era, faded into history's nether land. Joe died in 1967.

Story Notes

As an avid reader of history and watcher of the History Channel, I was always intrigued by the story of Joe Angelo. His story reinforces that one person can make an impact in a person's life and change history.

Chapter 9

The Fighting Quaker:
Smedley Darlington Butler

Not only is he a national hero, Smedley Butler is also a Marine Corps legend. He is the general who spoke out against big business in war. He is also one of the very few men in history to be a double recipient of the Medal of Honor.

Not many Americans today know the name Smedley Darlington Butler. Some might snicker at the strange-sounding name but not those who are or were marines. His name is held in reverence as one of the Marine Corps' greatest heroes. Even humorist Will Rogers claimed that Butler was a natural born warrior, adding that he admired him immensely.

There is, indeed, a great deal about Smedley Butler to admire. He was born in West Chester County, Pennsylvania, on July 30, 1881. His parents were Pennsylvania Quakers. His father was U.S. Congressman Thomas Stalker Butler. His mother Maude Darlington Butler taught him to be tolerant, truthful, and honest. These concepts were instilled in him not only at home but also in the weekly "Friends Meetings" he attended. Quaker beliefs range from the very conservative Evangelical to very liberal. They believe that an element of God's spirit exists in all human souls. To most Quakers, true religion is a personal encounter with God rather than ritual and ceremony.

Ironically, Smedley Butler became a warrior when the tenants of his religion called for pacifism, simplicity, and inner revelation; yet it's important to bear in mind that individualism within the religion is also encouraged. And if ever there was an individualist, Butler was one. Throughout his life, Smedley Butler spoke his mind. He didn't believe in lying to anyone for any reason. This trait earned him great respect and a few enemies.

Remember the *Maine*

Like the rest of America, Butler was outraged when on February 15, 1898, the battleship *Maine* blew up and sank in Havana Harbor. The *Maine* had been sent to Havana to protect life and property after riots rocked the city weeks earlier. Those who witnessed the event reported that the explosion lifted the ship out of the water while debris and human remains rained down into the water. The explosion occurred in the forward area of the ship that contained over 5,000 tons of powder. Over 260 sailors died. The blast was blamed on Spanish saboteurs or a mine; and this incident proved to be the catalyst that led the United States to declare war on Spain.

When the Spanish American War broke, Butler ran away from home and, lying about his age, joined the Marine Corps. All thoughts of pacifism vanished for young Smedley when the Marine Corps selected, trained, and commissioned him as 2nd Lieutenant in May 1898.

Like thousands of others, the 16-year-old Butler joined with the battle cry of "Remember the Maine" ringing in their ears. They joined the military to fight against an enemy who they believed led an unprovoked attack that killed hundreds of Americans.

Upon completion of his training, Butler was ordered to Guantanamo, Cuba, during what became known as the Spanish American War. He was assigned to Huntington's First Marine Battalion, Company B.

Second Lieutenant Smedley Butler soon learned about not judging people by appearance. During his time in Cuba, he and another two companions came across several dirty and disheveled marines sitting on some boxes. Butler immediately began to chew the men out for not snapping to attention when he came into their midst, for he was now an officer and a gentleman. He then demanded to know Lieutenant Colonel Huntington's location. That's when young Butler was informed that he was talking to Colonel Huntington, who then proceeded to chew the teenaged lieutenant up one side and down the other. Huntington then promptly put Butler to work learning how to perform nightly inspections of picket outposts.

Butler had arrived in Cuba too late to see any action, but he learned a lesson in humility that he never forgot. After returning to the United States, Huntington's Battalion was disbanded, and on February 16, 1899, Butler was honorably discharged from the Corps. Two months later he reapplied to the Marine Corps, and they again commissioned him a 2nd Lieutenant, this time assigning him to the 1st Marine Division in Manila, Philippine Islands, just before his 18th birthday.

For the next two years young Butler received his "baptism by blood and fire" in numerous actions during the Philippine American War. After the

Philippines, Butler was assigned to the 6th Marines and sent to China during the Boxer Rebellion of 1900.

On July 13, 1900, during a battle near the city of Tientsin, he and five others risked their lives to save a wounded allied soldier; Butler was seriously hurt. Ten days later, while still recovering, Lieutenant Smedley Butler was decorated for bravery; he received a battlefield promotion to brevet (brevet was a temporary wartime rank) captain.

After being gone for three years Butler returned to U.S. soil, but only until 1903 when the Marine Corps ordered him to protect the U.S. Consulate in Honduras. While there, he engaged Honduran rebels who attacked the consulate. No U.S. lives were lost, and Butler again returned home. In1905, he married Ethel C. Peters in Philadelphia, Pennsylvania, and settled into a calmer lifestyle.

After almost seven continuous years of military action, Captain Butler now held various posts in the United States, including commanding Marine Guards on various navy ships. But Smedley Butler craved something more. After all, he was a combat marine, and combat builds adrenaline, and human adrenaline can be very addictive. A true marine, Butler went where his country asked him to go, whether it was a navy ship or a hot spot in the world. He didn't have to wait long for that "hot spot" to arrive.

An Exemplary Military Career

In 1914, after being promoted to the rank of major, Butler was ordered to command a Marine regiment headed for Vera Cruz, Mexico. Political unrest threatened the lives of American citizens in that country. Butler, along with 800 marines and sailors, debarked from the battleship the USS *Texas* to occupy the city and protect the Americans living there and their businesses.

On April 22, 1914, Butler engaged superior Mexican forces; and according to records "was eminent and conspicuous in command of his Battalion. He exhibited courage and skill in leading his men through the action of the 22nd and in the final occupation of the city" (Medal of Honor Citations). For his action, Major Smedley Darlington Butler was awarded this nation's highest award for valor, the Medal of Honor.

Butler felt honored and yet strangely undeserving about receiving this medal, but his military career did not end the recognition. An incident a year and a half later cast him into the pantheon of Marine Corps legend. In October 1915, Smedley Butler and his marines were sent to Haiti to protect the country's Dictator Vilbrun Guillaume Sam against Caco rebels who sought to overthrow his regime.

On the night of the 24th, 400 Caco rebels ambushed Butler and his force of 44 mounted marines. Butler immediately barked out commands to his men to maintain their perimeter, and maintain they did throughout the night. With the first morning light, Butler ordered his men to attack the much larger force from three directions. This action totally surprised and shocked the Haitian rebels, who fled in panic.

The fighting wasn't over. For the next three weeks, skirmishes broke out, and pitched battles ensued. It all culminated on November 17, 1915. The Haitian rebellion had mostly been suppressed. The remaining Haitian rebels had taken refuge in an old French-built fort, deep within the mountains. Some of the marine officers argued that their existing forces could not take the fort. The front of the fort was only accessible by a very steep slope. Many felt that not only were they undermanned to charge from that position but also that they needed artillery support. Butler, though, convinced his colonel to let him lead the attack on the fort with less than 100 men and two machine gun detachments.

On the morning of November 17, 1915, with a small force that was outnumbered two to one, Major Butler moved into position. During his preparation–attack reconnaissance of the area, he discovered a seemingly impregnable drainage ditch on west wall of the fort. But Butler and two of his men crawled into the interior of the fort through this drainage ditch and began shooting, engaging the stunned defenders into brutal hand-to-hand combat. Butler then signaled the rest of his troops. His diversion allowed the rest of his marines to storm the fort. His forces charged the old French fort, and secured it after killing all 200 Caco rebels. Butler's marines suffered no casualties except for one man who lost two teeth after being struck in the mouth by a rock.

The two marines who crawled through the drainage ditch with Smedley, Private Samuel Gross and Sergeant Ross Iams, were awarded with the Medal of Honor and the Haitian Medal of Honor.

For his role, Butler was awarded with a second Medal of Honor from Franklin Delano Roosevelt, the assistant secretary of the Navy, making him only one of 19 men in U.S. history to become a double recipient of the award. His citation in part reads:

As Commanding Officer of detachments from the 5th, 13th, 23d Companies and the marine and sailor detachment from the U.S.S. Connecticut, Maj. Butler led the attack on Fort Riviere, Haiti, November 17, 1915. Throughout this perilous action, Maj. Butler was conspicuous for his bravery and forceful leadership. (Medal of Honor Citations)

The Caco bandits' efforts to retreat were cut off through a concentrated drive by the marines on the old French bastion fort. When the fighting ended,

Butler remained in Haiti, where he organized and commanded the newly established Haitian Gendarmerie, the native police force. As administrator, he supervised and restored many of the vital public works projects that had been interrupted by the rebellion.

The War to End All Wars

While Butler fought in Haiti, WWI raged in Europe. America was on the brink of entering the war after the *Lusitania* was sunk off the coast of Ireland only six months earlier.

When America finally entered the war in 1917, Butler, now a lieutenant colonel, inundated the navy department with requests for a combat command. Initially he was sent as a commander with the 13th Marines. Unfortunately for Butler, during WWI, the marines in Europe fell under the command of the U.S. Army. Butler's reputation as a fighter and double recipient of the Medal of Honor preceded him. Jealousy's venomous fangs bared themselves when senior army officers labeled Butler "a loose cannon" and worked hard to prevent him from commanding a combat unit.

However, General John J Pershing stepped in and personally ordered Butler to take command of the main American replacement depot—Camp Pontanezen in Brest. Butler was initially dismayed at the assignment. Some 100,000 troops packed together in this pest-infested mud hole. The sanitation facilities were so poor that an average of 25 servicemen died every day from causes such as influenza, dysentery, and cholera.

As disgusted as he was about this command, Butler attacked the job with vigor. Within weeks, he turned the camp into an orderly and efficient military camp. Because of his efforts, ability to organize, and because of the discipline and cleanliness, Butler instilled in the behavior of the men, the death rate of the camp significantly dropped.

The bright spot of this command was that the commander of the camp had to be at least a brigadier general; thus, for him to take command, Butler was promoted making him the youngest general officer in the Marine Corps. He was only 37 years old.

At the war's end, Camp Pontanezen became America's central debarkation depot. General Butler was awarded Distinguished Service Medals from both the Army and the Navy, as well as the French Order of the Black Star for his bravery as a accomplished leader. Shortly after the war, Butler looked back at his time in Vera Cruz, Mexico, in 1914. He felt that far too many Medals of Honor were handed out for the small campaign. His integrity forced him to write to his superiors to complain. He insisted on sending his medal back, because he felt undeserving. This is probably the only time in history that a Medal of Honor recipient tried to give his medal back.

His request was not only promptly denied, but he was also ordered to wear it or its ribbon on his uniform whenever he was in uniform.

A Legend Comes Home

After Butler returned to the United States, he was posted at the Marine Corps Base at Quantico, Virginia; and he served as the commanding general. Again, Butler initiated changes in training and discipline. Already a legend, he was highly respected by all who ever served under him or with him. Naturally, Butler did have some critics, though, who called him "eccentric." Eccentric or not, Butler firmly believed that the essence of the Marine Corps was unending training and discipline. He knew that the marines were the first to go into battle as he had done for almost a quarter of a century. He witnessed firsthand the effect that great training had on discipline and morale from Cuba to Europe. He also knew from firsthand experience that training could save lives in combat.

Smedley Butler also believed that any good commander would never ask his men to do something he would not himself do. In 1921, he personally led many of the field training exercises he ordered. During one such action he and his men were on farmland property that bordered the Ellwood plantation in the eastern edge of Orange County, Virginia. The area was the site of one of the most famous incidents in Civil War history.

It wasn't just that it was an historic battle site; it was also a burial site—one of the most unusual, if not the most unusual in American history. Here it was that, on the night of May 3, 1862, Confederate General Thomas "Stonewall" Jackson was accidentally shot by his own troops. In the darkness a volley of shots rang out and three musket balls struck Jackson. Two of them shattered his left arm. His men removed him to the plantation house so that the army surgeon could look after him. In the early morning hours, Jackson's left arm was amputated. In an attempt to save his life, his aides and the surgeon transported Jackson over 26 miles away to Guinea Station to catch a Richmond train. Jackson never made it. After all the efforts to save his life, he died of pneumonia.

Jackson's body was taken to Lexington, Virginia, where he was buried, but not quite all of him. Jackson's left arm was left at Ellwood Plantation, where it was buried in a grave with the inscription of "Arm of Stonewall Jackson, May 3, 1863." The legend of the arm being buried there flourished for almost 60 years until General Smedley Butler appeared with his marines.

Butler did not believe the legend. He ordered his men to dig up the grave to see if the arm was buried there; or if it were, in fact, a hoax. Much to his horror, this was no hoax. Lying there in front of him were skeletal remains of a human left arm!

Not wanting to desecrate the left arm's resting place any farther, Butler ordered that the arm be reburied. Then General Butler ordered that a bronze plaque be cemented to the top of the grave.

Endeavors at Home and Abroad

In 1924, General Smedley Butler took a leave of absence from the Marine Corps at the personal urging of the president of the United States. Butler was asked to become the Director of Public Safety for the City of Philadelphia, Pennsylvania—to clean up all of the corruption that infested the city. With the exception of Chicago and New York, Philadelphia was one of the most corrupt cities in the nation during the height of Prohibition. Butler took the job only with the condition that he would be able to return to the Marine Corps. Although he preferred the military, he carried out the job with the same zeal that he took in all of his commands in the Corps.

In his 11 months in Philadelphia, Smedley Butler stormed the city, much as he'd stormed the fort in Haiti. He took no prisoners in that he immediately rid the city of corrupt officials. He fired police captains, lieutenants, and raided speakeasies that serviced both the poor and the rich. In his fervor, Butler alienated a few too many judges and political bosses; and the mayor finally fired him. After returning to the Marine Corps, Butler purportedly claimed that cleaning up Philadelphia was worse than military action.

In 1927, the Marine Corps ordered Butler to command the Marine Expeditionary Forces. In the midst of a Chinese nationalist revolt, Butler's mission was to defend the American interests in Shanghai. The general executed his duties with such incredible diplomatic skills that the Chinese honored him with the ceremonial Umbrella of Ten Thousand Blessings not once, but twice—a truly amazing feat, as Butler was never one to be known for being diplomatic.

That became self-evident in 1931, when Major General Smedley Butler publicly told a story about Italian dictator Benito Mussolini striking a child with his automobile and leaving the scene. The story outraged the Italian counsel; they demanded an apology and Butler's arrest. Butler was court-martialed and ordered to apologize, as the Italians were friendly at the time. Of course, that would change in nine years.

Butler refused to apologize. The Italians were the only ones denying the story that the general had recalled. Why, thought Butler, should he apologize for telling the truth? On October 1, 1931, after 33 years of service, Butler decided to retire from his beloved Corps. He never stopped serving, though.

War Is a Racket

Two months before Butler's retirement in 1931, the American Legion conventions in New Britain, Connecticut, invited him to speak. In reflecting on his incredible career in the Marine Corps, Butler came to some startling conclusions. And he astonished his audience into silence when he began his speech saying, "I spent 33 years . . . being a high class muscle man for Big Business, for Wall Street and the bankers. In short, I was a racketeer for capitalism . . ."

He continued, speaking about his role in Nicaragua, Mexico, the Dominican Republic, Haiti and Cuba, as well as China; and the role big business played in those wars and conflicts. He accused Standard Oil's John D. Rockefeller, Brown Brothers, and other Wall Street firms, and J. P. Morgan of all being war profiteers. He accused steel companies, tire companies, and investment firms of making millions of dollars off the blood of the American soldier.

His speech so shocked his audience that few newspapers dared to print even part of it.

Butler's life had come full circle. He started out as a pacifist and Quaker, took a turn as a warrior, and now spoke out against war. He spoke publicly, insisting that war should only be fought in the defense of this country, and said that he was a firm believer in the Constitution of the United States and its Bill of Rights. He had sworn an oath to it when he was commissioned in the Marine Corps.

He also spoke out against fascism, and actively involved himself through publicly speaking out on behalf of this country's veterans, particularly during the Bonus March on Washington, D.C., in 1932. His loyalties were with these men. He became a writer and lecturer. Butler, expanded his speech and in 1935 published *War Is a Racket.* Since then over 300,000 copies have been sold.

A True Patriot Is Tested

But this isn't the end of Smedley Butler's story. His life took one more very strange turn that again cast him in history's spotlight.

In 1933, shortly after Franklin D. Roosevelt's inauguration, agents from several industrial giants approached Smedley Butler with an unbelievable plan. They wanted to overthrow the government of the United States—and they wanted Smedley Butler to help. They knew that Butler could muster support from millions of veterans, and they felt that he could mobilize an army of 500,000 soldiers overnight. They also knew that of all the war veterans in the public eye, Smedley Butler was most revered amongst America's fighting men.

The instigators of this plot suggested that all measures should be taken to overthrow the Roosevelt administration, including his murder if necessary. Their reason? Roosevelt's New Deal that was enacted during his first 100 days in office.

During the worst depression in American history, Roosevelt basically broke with the industrial giants to help average Americans. In Roosevelt's inaugural speech he proclaimed, "the only thing to fear is fear itself!" Roosevelt had awakened hope in the common person, but his policies scared and enraged bankers and industrialists—and now they wanted to get rid of the president.

The rich and powerful feared that they would lose a great deal of money. They felt the burden of paying for the New Deal would fall on their shoulders. They feared changes in the country's financial system, new taxes. Their biggest fear was that Roosevelt's policies would lead to Socialism and, thus, limit their profits. So they plotted a way to protect their fortunes by military overthrow of the government. When they approached Smedley Butler, he listened carefully to their plans. He met with these men on more than one occasion before he made his move.

Once he had gotten the information he needed, Butler didn't waste any time. He took this story to the Congress of the United States and was sworn in to give testimony to the treason in which he had been asked to participate. In his testimony Butler named a dozen industrial giants of the time. Butler had been a marine for 33 years and loved his country. He would never stand for anyone or any group that tried to overthrow the democracy he had fought to preserve. Investigations followed through major hearings (U.S. House, 1934).

The results of those hearings were controversial. Some reports say the industrialists were never charged with treason, because Roosevelt used them to push through the "New Deal." Other reports challenge the validity of some of the findings and claim there was a cover up to protect these business giants. What is known is recorded in the congressional hearings. What is also known is that many of these men adhered to fascism, and supported fascist tyrants like Benito Mussolini and Adolph Hitler before America's entrance into WWII.

Smedley Butler abhorred fascists, and everything for which they stood. Until his dying day, the general believed in democracy and the Constitution of the United States.

Up until the end of WWII, Major General Smedley Darlington Butler remained the most decorated marine in U.S. history. In his 33-year-old career as a marine, he had been involved in over 120 battles in places from Cuba, to China and from Mexico to the Philippines as well as Haiti and Nicaragua. He always held his oath to his country above all things, including now, when he questioned big business's involvement in and profit from the wars that young men fought to fill the coffers of Wall Street investors.

Even when, during the years between 1931 until 1940, he returned to his Quaker roots as a pacifist, Smedley Darlington Butler never stopped fighting for his country, upholding its Constitution and abiding by his principles. In 1940, Butler died of cancer at the Naval Hospital in Philadelphia. He is buried at Oakland Cemetery, West Chester, Pennsylvania.

Story Notes

I first heard the story of Smedley Butler from a friend of mine who was a marine and a combat Vietnam veteran. After hearing this story, I began researching him and was amazed at how little is told about this extraordinary man in today's history text books. Butler's book War Is a Racket *is fascinating because of the times in which he spoke out against war profiteering. The U.S. Marine Corps Museum in Quantico, Virginia, has chronicled this marine icon's life in detail.*

Chapter 10

A Miracle in the Trenches:
Robert Hulse

Robert E. Lee once said, "What a cruel thing is war: to separate and destroy families and friends, and mar the purest joys and happiness God has granted us in this world; to fill our hearts with hatred instead of love for our neighbors, and to devastate the fair face of this beautiful world" (http://ushistorysite.com/robert_e_lee_quotes.php). In 1914, an extraordinary event happened in the war-torn trenches of Belgium—a spontaneous peace broke out in the War to End all Wars.

It cannot be denied that throughout history, young men have always answered the call to duty and responded to the promise of adventure, wild times, and women. Through it all, most lost their innocence as witnesses to war's carnage, while some lost their limbs and lives. Even others lost their minds.

Another fact of life is that since time immemorial, young men have always fought the wars that old men started. While some of those wars were justified to protect countries from enemy attacks or invasion, others were the result of an extended family feud. In many ways, WWI was exactly that. All the European heads of state involved were related to each other either by blood or marriage, with a lineage that started with England's Queen Victoria's nine children.

Kaiser Wilhelm II of Germany was the queen's eldest grandson and the one she thought the most dangerous for the stability of Europe. In June 1914, with the assassination of Austria's Archduke Franz Ferdinand added to a backdrop of European political intrigue, the Kaiser ignited WWI. It seems the old queen wasn't far off in her assessment of her grandson and she had that feeling about him years before her death in 1901.

But then again, Victoria's English heirs were no angels either. This was a time of unbridled imperialism, when European heads of state used any means to conquer and dominate others. In fact, the British Empire was the largest in the world. British colonies included parts of Asia, Africa, and Canada, as well as all of India and Australia.

Now England and her allies were at war with Germany, each seeking to expand their empires.

The slaughter of WWI began in Belgium in August 3, 1914, when German troops crossed the border between Holland and France and completely destroyed the Belgian's small army. In less than three weeks they occupied Brussels. In the next few months, the savagery and the war escalated into proportions that were unbelievable to both sides. It was so far reaching, so brutal, and vicious that WWI became known as the "War to End All Wars." Reports of it horrified the "civilized" world.

From the beginning, this war was different from those that preceded it—especially in the ways in which it was fought. The machine gun was used extensively for the first time; and hundreds of miles of trenches that men dug and died in crisscrossed France and Belgium's countryside.

The United States sought to remain neutral, and did so until the luxury ocean liner the SS *Lusitania* was sunk by a German submarine off the coast of Ireland on May 1, 1915.

Of the 1,159 people who died, 123 were Americans. This tragedy outraged the people of the United States, and many began to think that neutrality was no longer an option; while at the same time, news reports of the carnage in Europe made others think twice about having America's young men and women go off to fight in the trenches of France and Belgium. Still, three and a half years after it started, America entered the war, mainly because of business interests with England and France, and the unrestricted submarine warfare the Germans had unleashed on all shipping.

Popular support for the war was won with the help of patriotic songs like George M. Cohan's "Over There." Most Americans were convinced that once U.S. troops landed, the war would be short lived.

Yet, it wasn't until May 1918 that American servicemen saw their first combat action. Within the six months of the "doughboy's" arrival, close to 117,000 Americans were killed and twice as many were wounded. Those six months also introduced America to men who would become legends, not only on the battlefield but also in the years that followed.

Sergeant Alvin C. York became America's most decorated hero when he single handedly captured 132 German soldiers on October 8, 1918. Meanwhile the aerial exploits of Captain Eddie Rickenbacker, "America's Ace of Aces," became legendary after he shot down 26 German planes. For their actions in combat, both Rickenbacker and York received America's highest award for valor, the Medal of Honor.

Other WWI figures who became larger-than-life historic figures as well include Captain Harry S Truman, who eventually became president of the

United States in WWII following the death of President Franklin D. Roosevelt and General Douglas MacArthur, who became general of the Army during WWII.

One of America's greatest writers, Ernest Hemingway, was an ambulance driver for the Italian Army. His best-selling book, *A Farewell to Arms* was loosely based on his WWI experience.

But even before America entered the war, for 10 brief days, there was a glimmer of hope—a glimmer of hope that was lit by the kind of war heroes who are not remembered in the history books. It happened on December 24, 1914. There are many versions of this event told by the men. The last survivor of the truce, Sergeant Alfred Anderson from Scotland, died at the age of 109 in 2005. From their small actions, something incredible happened that night (*New York Times*, 2005).

It all started out with the faint sounds of the song "Silent Night, Holy Night" on that cold Christmas eve. The song soon became ubiquitous from where another soldier, Edward Hulse, was lying. For Hulse's companions began singing too, but in a different language!

It was all too surreal for the 25-year-old Hulse. Then one of his astonished companions saw a man walking toward them with a small, candle-lit spruce tree. Like a ghost the figure moved in the winter night, barely silhouetted by the tree's light. Hulse's first thoughts were incredulous; "just what the hell was going on?"

The man walking toward him was wearing a gray coat, and in broken English said, "This is for you and your companions." The man in the gray coat explained that in his country, this tree was used to celebrate the Christmas holiday and since this was Christmas eve, he wanted to share the tradition.

As the man with tree was speaking, dozens of other gray phantoms began appearing and walking toward Hulse and his companions. Their hands grasped only winter's air above their heads. Almost simultaneously Hulse's companions moved up from their positions to greet these men in peace—these same men they had been trying to kill for the past five months, in that year of 1914.

These were German soldiers without deception or malice, crossing over the mantle of dead that lay in the fields of "No Man's Land." In the winter night these Germans journeyed through that area that separated their trenches from those of the British, just 50 yards away, to wish their enemy "Merry Christmas." And now with their bare hands, they reached out to greet the living in friendship. Stiffened hands reached out from all directions, imploring the living to stop the madness.

Without orders from those who start wars, peace had broken out amongst those who cherish it more than anyone. Yes, there would be peace that night and into the next day and into the next week. The first thing these men would do, though, was to bury their dead.

Both British and Germans helped each other in digging graves and attending funeral services on Christmas morning. Then they began exchanging gifts. More impromptu concerts of the season were sung throughout the front lines in German and English. German sausage was shared, while buttons, coins, pipes, and insignias were exchanged. Hats and helmets were swapped as other men bartered for cigarettes and German cigars. British rum was traded for French cognac or wine. And with each beverage there was a pledge to each other's health. Photos of loved ones, fingered with affection, were shown in common adoration, and passed from hand to hand. Questions such as "how old is your child?" and "how long have you been married?" and "where did you meet you wife or girl friend?" were asked. And when it was learned that there were barbers among the enemy, they shaved a number of men, including Edward Hulse, in No Man's Land.

Later on that Yuletide day, someone produced a homemade soccer ball; and combat in the form of sport broke out. The Germans defeated the "Brits" by one goal. The Brits claimed it was because the field judge was German. But they laughed and joked about it during death's brief respite. And they continued to speak of home, sweethearts, and of common places they had been.

One German had worked in England before the war only two doors down from a shop that one of the English soldier's father owned. Another German had worked in a Berlin restaurant that was a favorite of English officers before the war. Soldiers on both sides learned too that the propaganda that taught them hate was untrue. Germans and British soldiers were the same, men who loved and who were loved by their families. They were not the monsters created by the hate of politicians. They had been taught to hate and how to dehumanize their enemy. Only then could they be taught how to kill.

The unofficial Christmas truce of 1914 lasted only 10 days. When word of this truce soon spread to military headquarters on both sides, it was determined that these actions would not be tolerated. England's and Germany's rulers and generals made sure that no more truces would be held in the battlefield without their consent. Peace would come only after the slaughter of their enemies. And they proclaimed it in the name of God and country, each "knowing" that God was on their side.

The orders were given. This was war; any man who disobeyed an order to fight would be severely punished or executed. Line officers would be held accountable for the actions or nonactions of their men.

At first the men on both sides fired their weapons sporadically but always high above the heads of any of the men with whom they had shared their 10 days of peace. On January 4 though, a British officer ordered the shooting death of a German who was in plain sight, near his own trenches. From that time on until November 11, 1918, the war dogs of hell were loosed. And they were loosed in the most hideous ways: poison gas. And for the first time in humankind's history, the tank and the airplane became weapons of carnage. During that time, in the war to end all wars, men were relentlessly slaughtered up and down those same trenches—except for during the Christmas truce.

Somewhere on that silent night, of December 24, 1914, a hero had leashed and muzzled the dogs of war from where they had freely roamed, only hours earlier. That someone was a common foot soldier who remembered the teachings of the Christ child. And they who knew whose side God was on, the side of Peace.

* * *

Five months later, the second Battle of Ypres began; and this time the carnage was even worse. The Germans began using chlorine gas. The shelling and machine gun fire constantly filled the air. Although Canadian doctor, Major John McCrae had been a combat physician for many years, he found it impossible to get used to the suffering he encountered on the combat field.

After losing a close friend and former student to a shell burst, McCrae had him buried near his aid station. The next day McCrae woke and saw the wild poppies that grew in and around the ditches of the countryside during that Belgium spring. In 20 minutes he wrote down one of the most famous war poems ever penned:

"In Flanders Fields"

In Flanders Fields the poppies blow
Between the crosses row on row,
That mark our place; and in the sky
The larks, still bravely singing, fly
Scarce heard amid the guns below.
We are the dead. Short days ago
We lived, felt dawn, saw sunset glow,
Loved and were loved, and now we lie
In Flanders Fields.
Take up your quarrel with the foe:
To you from failing hands we throw
The torch; be yours to hold it high.
If ye break faith with us who die
We shall not sleep, though poppies grow
In Flanders Fields.

—Lieutenant Colonel John McCrae

From the time that Major McCrae wrote "In Flanders Fields" the war raged on for another four years at the cost of 12 million lives. Another 18 million perished worldwide because of the flu virus that came from a U.S. Army post in

Kansas. Ironically, Dr. John McCrae fell victim to it in 1918, just before the war ended. The official cause of death was listed as pneumonia.

On the 11th hour of the 11th day of the 11th month in the year 1918, an armistice was signed to end, what was up till then, the world's worst war.

Story Notes

The first stories I heard about WWI came from a neighbor of mine. I remember his name as Hanley. In 1964, I remember his telling me that he had fought in the war that was supposed to end all wars back in 1918. He not only told me about his experiences but also that he'd been told of the Christmas Truce in 1914 a couple of years before he went to France.

On the day I was to leave my Denver home to report to Navy Boot Camp in San Diego, Mr. Hanley rang our doorbell. He told my mother he wanted to speak to me for a minute.

He informed me that he had come over to shake my hand and wish me well. He then told me a story about the day he left home to fight in France. It seems a neighbor of his came over to his house to shake his hand and wish him well. That neighbor, he said, was a Civil War veteran. It dawned on me that with two simple handshakes, we had crossed one hundred years of time with the same message.

Chapter 11

The Last Acoma:
Sam Antonio

When Sam Antonio was a young boy, fast food meant a rabbit. And being able to run a rabbit down took a great deal of speed and agility on Sam's part. Not only would he chase after the rabbit, but from the late spring to early autumn, he would also dodge the many rattlesnakes that made their homes in the desert. If Sam failed to catch a rabbit or two, it would mean a meatless meal or hunger for everyone in his household. Sam and his dog Hickquay rarely failed. They had the art of rabbit hunting down to such a precise art that Hickquay would find a rabbit and chase it toward Sam. Sam in turn had a long stick with notches carved on the tip. If the rabbit made its way past Sam and into a hole, Sam was able to take the stick and reach into the hole or behind the rocks and twist it into the rabbit's fur and was able to pull him out. Yes, Sam was fast; he grew up following the ancient ways of his Acoma (pronounced Ack Kah mah) people.

Sam Antonio and five other Acoma boys were inducted into the Army in the spring of 1940. As a matter of fact it was April Fools' Day. At first Sam thought it was a joke, but he realized it wasn't when four days later he and five other Acoma boys were sent to Fort Bliss, Texas, for basic training. Army life was totally foreign to Sam who had grown up with the Acoma way of life.

The troops were taught how to march and how to clean their ancient 1903 Springfield Rifles. Then they were taught to march again. And again. When they were shipped off to the Philippine Islands in August 1941, they became part of the 200th Coastal Artillery Unit from New Mexico. Sam's life would never again be the same.

When Sam Antonio was inducted into the U.S. Army, he never dreamed that he would become one of the "Battling Bastards of Bataan." Nor would he have ever dreamed that he would spend three and a half years in a Japanese prisoner-of-war (POW) camp in Manchuria. He didn't think of these things because his mother had assured him that he and his three brothers would all come back from the war alive. And yet her prediction was odd because, at that time, there was no war. Nevertheless, she blessed Sam before he left for basic training. This was not an unusual thing for Sam's mother to do, for everyone in the Pueblo knew that she was a powerful medicine woman. They knew she had cured many of her own people of illnesses white doctors said were terminal and that she could see into the future on occasion. And she had seen a war coming.

Sam grew up not far from Grants, New Mexico, near the ancient Acoma Pueblo, known as Sky City. It is the oldest pueblo in the United States where people have continually lived for over 600 years. Within sight of this pueblo is the Enchanted Mesa, which was where the Acoma had first placed their village. The Acoma say that they once lived high on that rock, while down below they farmed in the fertile grasslands. There was only one way to the village and it was up a very steep incline. One day though, there was either a terrible earthquake or thunderstorm that destroyed the pathway to the village. It was said that those on top of the rock starved to death and those who were down below created Sky City. This was the story handed down through the centuries. And from this and other stories, Sam learned how his people prayed to the dawning sun and the setting sun each day. He spoke only his native language of Acoma until he was seven years old. That was when the county sheriff came.

Sam and others had now reached school age and Bureau of Indian Affairs (BIA) regulations stated that all children of school age would be sent to Indian boarding school, which involved being taken from their homes—sometimes forcibly. Sam was sent to school in Santa Fe, New Mexico; and for the next few years he lived and went to school there. He was allowed home visit only on holidays and summer breaks. Boarding school did all it could to take the "Indian" out of Sam and the others who were there. They were taught to speak English, and how to read and write, and were punished if they spoke their own language or worshipped in their own religion.

Sam's treatment at the school taught him that the ways of his own people was more compassionate than the "civilized world" into which he was thrust. Sam kept his culture alive by speaking in Acoma to the others from his reservation. And he continued praying to the rising and setting sun, as his people had for a thousand years.

In 1936, Sam was allowed to go back to his home where he was one of the first Native Americans who attended public high school in Grants, New Mexico. His natural ability for sports allowed him to excel in all that he tried: baseball, basketball, football, and track. Because of his early training in chasing down rabbits, Sam became one of the fastest 880 yards runners in New Mexico; but it was his boxing ability that won him an Amateur Athletic Union (AAU) National Championship in 1939 in the 118-pound featherweight division.

After Sam graduated from school, he went to work for the railroad in Grants. One day he saw a familiar face in the rail yards. It was a Lakota friend of his that he knew from his days in boarding school. They talked for a while when he asked Sam what he was doing there. Sam explained that he was working for the railroad. His friend laughed and said that he was riding the rails. He was a hobo. "Sam," he said. "Why don't you come ride the rails with me? It's a great adventure and I'll teach you all you need to know" (Antonio, 1984–2004).

It sounded good to Sam and without hesitation, he and his friend caught the next train out of Grants for points unknown. There were no goodbyes to anyone; he just left New Mexico on the hobo trail. For weeks he traveled with people of all races who lived the hobo life. At each stop they all had two important jobs: first, don't get caught by the "bulls" (the law), and second, scrounge up some food to share with everyone in camp. When the opportunity presented itself, Sam would catch a rabbit. Sam didn't know it at the time but some of this training would help save his life two years later.

As the weeks went by, Sam finally got homesick and decided to go back to New Mexico. All the time he was gone, his family didn't know whether he was alive or dead. When he arrived home, his angry but thankful mother asked him where he'd been. After he told her his story, she asked, "Why didn't you write?" Without hesitation Sam answered, "Because I knew you didn't know how to read." Realizing what Sam had said was true, she laughed, but added, "But your sister could have read it to me" (Antonio, 1984–2004).

When basic training was over Sam and the others stayed on at Fort Bliss for artillery training. They became part of the 200th Coastal Artillery Unit from New Mexico and were shipped off to the Philippine Islands in August 1941.

Sam found the islands beautiful with it lush jungles and exotic plants and birds. Coming from the deserts of New Mexico, the crystal clear Pacific waters were an incredible sight. Mangos were ripe and plentiful, as were coconuts and bananas. But the poverty and simple lifestyle of the friendly Filipino people, amid the world of whites, reminded Sam of his own people. Of course, within four months, all this would change and with it, the Philippines, the world, and Sam's life.

On December 8, 1941, the day after the attack on Pearl Harbor, the Japanese invaded the Philippines. Sam and the others first heard the planes outside of their billeted area near Clark Field, not far from Manila, and they ran outside to see who was flying over. The planes were flying too high to identify, but one of the men in Sam's group counted 54. At first they all thought the planes were U.S. naval flyers. That was before the first bombs began falling around them and on to Clark Field. High-level Japanese bombers struck the planes of U.S. Army Air Corps forces on the ground. Eighteen of 35 B-17 bombers and 56 fighters were destroyed in the initial attack.

Sam and the others were horrified. They had heard the news of Pearl Harbor, but they didn't expect the war to reach them so quickly and with such devastation. The next day the U.S. Navy pulled its Asiatic Fleet out of the Philippines and the remaining B-17s flew south to Australia. Small Japanese landing parties began debarking on the Philippine Islands and then from December 22nd and 23rd the main invasion groups landed.

General Douglas MacArthur ordered all U.S. military units to retreat to the Bataan Peninsula. They accomplished this in a leapfrog manner. One unit would protect another's retreat and another would in turn protect them. The inexperienced troops brilliantly executed this maneuver until the 80,000 men and their artillery gained the peninsula by January 6, 1942.

Sam and others fought in the immense jungles of the Philippines day after day waiting for what General Douglas MacArthur had promised in his letter of January 15, 1942:

> . . . Help is on the way from the United States. Thousands of troops and hundreds of planes are being dispatched. The exact time of arrival of reinforcements is unknown as they will have to fight their way through Japanese against them. It is imperative that our troops hold until these reinforcements arrive. No further retreat is possible . . . I call upon every soldier in Bataan to fight in his assigned position, resisting every attack. This is the only road to salvation. . . . (Moore, 2004, p. 46)

Everyone knew MacArthur's words were inspiring, but everyone also knew that it would be a matter of time before they were overrun by the Japanese if help did not arrive soon. But there was no help. The Pacific fleet had been destroyed. American and Filipino military forces in the Philippines were greatly outgunned though not outmanned. For the next three months they gave ground, but they made the Japanese pay for it in blood. The following two months, they took everything the Imperial Japanese Army threw at them, but finally, on April 8, 1941, Bataan fell. On the next day most of its defenders surrendered. They were out of food and almost totally out of ammunition.

Though the Americans outnumbered the invading army, they didn't have modern rifles or tanks to hold them back. But Sam and the other defenders of the Bataan Peninsula held out for five months. They were finally forced to surrender. He and thousands of others became victims of the infamous Bataan Death March.

Sam and the other survivors waited by the beach at Mariveles, on the southern tip of the peninsula. One of the men in Sam's unit saw a boat out on the water. If he and others could reach it they might be able to make to Corregidor. Sam and seven others made the trip on two boats. One of the boats was small craft that Sam had scrounged. To the south of them, across about three miles of open ocean, lay the island of Corregidor. The Americans, now under the command of General Jonathan Wainwright (General MacArthur had been ordered out of the Philippines by President Roosevelt) still held the island.

Sam and the others were the lucky ones. Day turned into night as they paddled for over nine hours in shark-infested waters. They finally made it to Corregidor and successfully avoided the Japanese troops that had already landed on that island. Those who could not make it off the Bataan were forced to surrender on that day.

After surrendering, some 75,000 U.S. soldiers and Philippine scouts were force marched from Mariveles, in the south, to a railroad siding at San Fernando 40 miles away. Many of these men had already come down with malaria and dysentery from lack of proper food and medical attention. The infamous death march had begun.

The Japanese denied these men all food and water under the blinding tropical sun and if a prisoner fell down from exhaustion, he was either shot or bayoneted. If a prisoner spoke out, he was viciously beaten or killed. Once in awhile a Japanese office would test how sharp his samurai sword was by randomly cutting off the head of prisoner who was straggling from formation. An estimated 7,000–10,000 men died; 2,000 of them were Americans, on this march to the first of many POW camps. Sam would not be one of them (Camp O'Donnell, 1945).

Through courage seldom seen in the face of such overwhelming odds Sam and the others had proudly earned their nickname "The Battling Bastards of Bataan." Those who did not get off the Bataan that day were now at the mercy of their captors—captors who, just a couple of years earlier, had murdered thousands of Manchurian civilians.

Sam and those who made it to Corregidor would only know freedom for 27 days. On May 6, 1942, General Jonathan Wainwright surrendered to an overwhelming enemy. Sam was taken prisoner. Though he would try time and again, there would be no escape.

From December 1941 until General Wainwright's surrender in May 1942, Sam Antonio witnessed incredible feats of heroism. On more than one occasion he saw Filipino cavalry chasing Japanese tanks with their horses. If they could get up along side of the tank, they would pull the pin of a grenade and try to toss it into the tank's hatch. On more than one occasion they succeeded. Some of those men lived to tell about it. For those who did not, Sam tells their story for them.

A new roundup of prisoners began after General Wainwright surrendered his forces. Many of the men had hoped for some decent food, for they had been eating snakes, monkeys, and iguanas for the past couple of months. The running joke was that the government issues (GIs) had made all of the snakes and iguanas extinct species in Bataan and Corregidor. But the decent food and care would not come. After Sam and the others were herded up, the commander of the Imperial Japanese Army in the Philippines General Homa came to the great tunnel fortress of Corregidor to take Wainwright's formal surrender. All the prisoners were ordered to observe the ceremony and salute or bow down to General Homa and the flag of Japan. But Sam and a friend, Jose Isidro Cata, a Pueblo Indian from the San Juan Pueblo, New Mexico, slipped away and hid underneath a truck that had been destroyed during the fighting.

There beneath that truck, in the hot tropical sun, Sam Antonio made a vow that he would not bow down or salute that flag. For in his Acoma ways, though Sam had always prayed to the morning sunrise, he'd be damned if he would bow or salute to the flag of the "rising sun." Sam was not caught that day, but he had nowhere to escape so he rejoined the main body of his unit. Then the looting started.

Japanese guards began moving through the ranks and taking anything of value from the prisoners: rings, watches, necklaces, and wallets. If a prisoner refused he was severely beaten or killed. The Japanese used pillow cases to hold all their loot.

Then the Japanese began to separate Americans and Filipino scouts. Sam and others from his unit and others were separated and taken to the coast. They were to be shipped away from the Philippines to points unknown. They didn't know whether they were going to be killed. They were taken from Corregidor, by ship, back to Bataan and unloaded. On their march to Manila, Sam and the others were amazed at the greetings that came from the Filipino people. They were astounded that Sam and the other Americans were still alive. From the side of the roads, the gathering of Filipinos threw out cigarettes, candy, bananas, rice balls, and money. Americans who fell from exhaustion were helped to their feet by the Filipinos. The Japanese did not interfere. The crowds thinned out as Sam and the others continued to march to a prison camp called Bilibid. For the next few weeks conditions were horrible. It got worse when they were sent to another prison camp called Cabanatuan.

The Americans were marched from Bilibid to a rail yard and literally crammed into box and cattle cars like sardines without oil. The smell of sweat and human waste was to become common. Fights broke out for space in the cramped cars and two more Americans died. The Japanese told the prisoners that if any more trouble broke out they would kill 10 men. The prisoners tried to get any comfort they could find as they traveled until they reached their destination Cabanatuan.

Sam and the other prisoners were taken off the train and marched a short distance to the Cabanatuan schoolyard. It had been converted into a temporary prison. They were given food, water, and rest. For on the next day they would start on a 12-mile march. The march took hours in the fly-infested heat. Again stragglers were beaten and prodded with bayonets until they finally reached their destination. The only good thing to greet Sam was the other five Acomas who had been in his unit. All six men had survived up to that point. From July until October the Americans lived in extremely primitive conditions. They had no bathrooms. What they did have was a long ditch in which water ran through the camp. It was called a "straddle-sleuth." If a man had to relieve himself, he would straddle the ditch to do so. Many men were so weak that when the attempted this they would fall in. Some died there. In October, word had gone out that a select few men (about a thousand of them) were to be shipped out of Cabanatuan to Manila. They were going to be sent out of the Philippines. Sam would be among those chosen.

The prisoners were told they were going to be marched to Manila. But something was very different in the way that they were treated on this march to the coast. They weren't beaten, shot, stabbed, or abused in anyway. And their march was not a forced one, as had been the case only months back. Once they reached Manila they were taken to Pier 7 where pots of steamed rice awaited them. Food! Food was always on their minds. Food and escape took over all of their thoughts. Sam and the others waited for two days before they met another group of American prisoners from another camp. There were about 2,000 men who awaited the Japanese freighter *Hokka Maru*. They were told that they were going to Manchuria. They were to be workers in the machine shops and mills there to support the Japanese war machine.

Once the ship arrived, the prisoners were put below decks. Again, there was no room for anyone. And again there were no bathroom facilities aboard this ship. After the first few hours at sea, the lower decks were covered with feces, urine, and vomit and there was no fresh air. Some men went to the main deck of the ship, risking death to the squalor below. Sam was confined below. While he was down there the *Hokka Maru* became a target of an American or British submarine. Two torpedoes were fired at the ship full of prisoners but fate intervened. Miraculously, this big clumsy ship was able to outmaneuver the sub's torpedoes and continued on to Formosa.

The sanitation conditions did not improve until the Japanese soldiers themselves started complaining about how bad the smells below were. Those who died in these wretched conditions were buried at sea. Fire hoses were finally brought down and the men and their quarters were sprayed alike.

After the *Hokka Maru* reached port in Formosa, the men were transferred to a newer freighter called the *Hokka Maru 2*. From there they sailed until they reached Fusan port in Korea. Sam and the others were then sent by rail to Manchuria. The name of their prison camp was Mukden.

For the next three and a half years, Sam was sent to work in the textile shop, making canvas in the fall and winter. But in the spring and summer months, Sam was put to work in fields as a farmer. He and the others planted a variety of food for the rest of the prisoners and the guards. This was a detail that Sam enjoyed because he got to eat when he wasn't supposed to. Carrots! He ate a lot of carrots to help keep away the ever-present pangs of hunger!

Throughout his three and a half years in Mukden, Sam continually tried to escape. During one attempt he accidentally came in contact with an electric fence. The force of the electricity violently threw him back to the ground. The man with him had to revive him. The burns he received were so severe that he burned off his fingerprints. (To this day, he jokes about how he could go out and commit a crime and get away with it. The reason for it, he says, is that the police would never be able to identify him through his fingerprints because he doesn't have any.) He and many other Americans at Mukden continually sabotaged the machines on which they worked. Most of the machines were American made and if they could put it out of commission the Japanese had no way of replacing broken parts.

In thinking back about the horrors of war and his imprisonment, Sam also remembered those who were kind to him, when their actions could have cost them their lives. There is a story of when he was struck by a Japanese guard. The guard thought Sam was making fun of him. Without thinking, Sam struck back at the guard, but fortunately, he did not make contact. That would have been an instant death sentence to Sam. The guard reported what had happened to an officer. Sam's punishment would be severe. Sam was made to stand at strict attention for 24 hours with a bayonet, attached to a rifle, placed upright, just under his chin. If he nodded off to sleep, his head would fall; and he would impale himself through his head. Sam stayed awake most of the time. He did start to nod off and that's how he stabbed himself through the chin just under his tongue. He still has the scar. Through war's profanity though, Sam found decency.

Two guards watching Sam through this ordeal saved his life. Secretively, they removed the bayonet for several hours allowing Sam to sleep during his ordeal. Without their help, Sam would not have lived to tell his story.

In August 1945, Sam and the other prisoners at Mukden knew something was finally happening. They could see and hear American airplanes flying overhead and there was almost no resistance from the Japanese. One time when the bombers came in to bomb the factories, one of the bombs went astray and landed in an American barracks. Nineteen U.S. prisoners who were with Sam in Mukden were killed!

Shortly thereafter, members of the Office of Strategic Services (OSS), the forerunner to today's Central Intelligence Agency (CIA), parachuted into the Mukden prison grounds to the shock of everyone there. They had come to tell the Japanese that the war was over. Two atomic bombs had been dropped on Japan itself. At first these Americans were not believed, but the Japanese knew that the Soviets were fast approaching Mukden. Within days they arrived and liberated the camp. Sam couldn't believe his eyes. Within the ranks of the Soviet troops were women. Some of them were officers and others were noncoms. They had fought with the men through China and had come to liberate Mukden.

Real food came in by the truckloads and the men who had been prisoners now watched as their captors were disarmed and imprisoned.

Sam and the other prisoners were finally freed, with Japan's surrender to allied forces. The U.S. Army finally gave Sam and the other soldiers of Bataan and Corregidor the Bronze Star medal with a "V" for valor. He and the others had earned many times over.

Sam still values those traditions taught to him by his mother and father. He has passed along much of that to his daughters and son. He hopes that his great-grandson "Little Sammy" will one day learn. There is a good chance of that because Sam's granddaughter Tina and "Little Sammy" live with him.

Story Notes

I first met Sam Antonio more than 20 years ago through his niece Teddy Duncan. She approached me at a storytelling program I was giving, and offered to arrange a meeting for me to talk to her uncle. It was one of the best things that had ever happened to me.

We became great friends. Sam told me that before he met me, he never talked to anyone about his imprisonment. For some reason, he decided to trust me and not only opened up to me with his story but also allowed me to share it in this collection.

Portions of this story are reprinted from Patrick Mendoza, Extraordinary People in Extraordinary Times: Heroes, Sheroes, and Villains. *Englewood, CO: Libraries Unlimited. Copyright © 1999 Patrick M. Mendoza.*

Chapter 12

The First Son and the Second Marines:
James Roosevelt and Carlson's Raiders

James Roosevelt and Evans F. Carlson played a pivotal part in changing a concept in Marine Corps warfare in the South Pacific during the first few months of WWII. The following story describes those months and the histories of the two men involved.

At 34 years of age, he was too old to be drafted, incredibly nearsighted and had flat feet, plus an assortment of other ailments that made him ineligible for active military service. He obviously didn't have to join the Marine Corps, the Navy, or even worry about being drafted into the Army. James Roosevelt was considered 4-F, physically unfit!

However, unlike the offspring many of today's politicians, Roosevelt used his considerable political influence to get *into* the Marine Corps! That influence took form in the shape of his father, Franklin Delano Roosevelt, the president of the United States.

Actually, this was the second time James Roosevelt became a marine.

James Roosevelt was the president's oldest son and aide. As such, he worked closely with his father during his political campaigns. He also physically cared for his ailing father's needs. The American public was unaware that the president had been stricken with poliomyelitis. He could not stand without the two heavy braces on his legs and James's aid.

James Roosevelt remembered,

Serving him, I was cursed by critics on charges of nepotism. I am, however, proud to have served him. I saw him crawl across the floor—a cripple practicing his escape from a fire, which never came. I helped him hobble up to platforms of power. And I laid him on the floor of a private railway car to rest at a time when his illness kept him from making the sort of public appearance expected of him. (Roosevelt, 1976, back cover jacket)

In 1936, James Roosevelt was made a Marine lieutenant colonel overnight with the stroke of a pen. While accompanying his father to Argentina aboard the USS *Indianapolis*, he was made a military aid. James later remembered, he didn't think anything of it at the time. Later though, he realized he didn't know anything about being a Marine lieutenant colonel so he resigned his commission.

In 1940, while living in Los Angeles, Roosevelt received a special waiver to join the Marine Reserves and was commissioned as a captain. Later that year his unit was activated. This time he went through Marine training like everyone else and earned his rank.

Roosevelt bypassed the prerequisite firsthand training in polishing brass. All Marine-enlisted men learned how. What this had to do with combat has remained a mystery since Brasso was invented. But it sure makes things look all pretty and shinny. This was also true for mastering the "spit shined" shoe. A marine performed this skill by applying black wax shoe polish on a shoe or boot with a soft rag mixed with either water or spit. This task took hours to produce a high-gloss shine, one in which you could see your face. All uniforms were immaculately pressed.

Roosevelt was, after all, an officer; and officers weren't required to perform such menial and boring tasks. In fact, his enlisted aides performed those tasks for him. That would all change after the attack on Pearl Harbor. For a while James Roosevelt was assigned to an intelligence unit, but he requested a transfer to a combat unit.

Marine Corps training differed from that of other ground troops. They were trained as amphibious ground troops, an elite force to be the first to go into combat. Roosevelt, like the other marines learned that the emphasis during training was on land combat. Hand-to-hand combat, bayonet drills, shooting skills as well as marching for endless hours were a major part of his training. That was hard for him because of his flat feet. The marines' credo was "knowing your job and the job of the guy next to you." If the chain of command was broken, the next marine in line was taught to take over. Each man knew how to complete the mission.

The leatherneck's bible was the *Marine Corps Field Manual*. Like the *Blue Jacket's Manual,* this book contained everything a marine needed to know about his chosen service. All they would have to do is practice and drill, and then drill some more after more practice; and then they might become a marine.

After boot camp, the recruit was sent to advanced infantry training, then to specialized training. Specialty training was always secondary to marine training for everyone.

Evans F. Carlson

In the fall of 1939, Evans Carlson resigned his commission in the Marine Corps, and began writing and lecturing throughout the United States about the dangers this country faced by the Japanese. He had been in China for the past two years and had witnessed the horrors the Japanese had inflicted upon the Chinese. And it was there he learned even more about guerilla warfare from the Red Chinese Army than he had learned in Nicaragua a few years earlier.

Evans F. Carlson, the son of a Congregationalist Church minister, had a long varied military career before WWII. He ran away from home at age 14. Two years later after lying about his age, Evans joined the U.S. Army. He served in WWI but saw no combat. He resigned from the Army after the war working as a salesman until 1922. He then reenlisted in the Marine Corps. Carlson then felt that he was in his element. Within five years he was sent to China with the 4th Marines. He served there for three years. And then he was sent to fight in Nicaragua. It was there, in that Central American country, that Carlson first encountered guerilla warfare. This trademark style of fighting was centuries old. The natives had used it with the Spanish and now used with the American marines. This experience only sparked Carlson's interest in this type of warfare. It would not be his last encounter with guerilla fighting.

As a 1st Lieutenant, Carlson led 12 marines against 100 bandits and for this action he was awarded his first Navy Cross, the highest award for valor the Navy and Marine Corps can bestow. Carlson was further commended for his actions following a major earthquake in that country in 1931 and for his role as chief of police in Managua until 1933.

After repeated trips to China and Japan, Carlson predicted that this country was headed for war with Japan and that they would attack Pearl Harbor in May or June 1941. He was wrong by only six months.

On the other side of the world, Marine Lieutenant Colonel Evans F. Carlson approached President Roosevelt, whom he had known, to obtain permission to form a combat organization, unlike anything the Marine Corps had at the time. It would be an elite fighting force within the already-elite Marine Corps.

His idea comprised of a special force of men trained for arduous but, swift marches. It would be radio equipped. Each man carried a large number of automatic weapons. And they learned to live on tasteless dehydrated foods. Both he and James Roosevelt, the president's son, worked hard on the game plan.

Carlson's plan further ended the traditional officers' privileges. Each officer dressed as an enlisted man, carried his own equipment, and lived as an enlisted man. Once this plan was approved, the officers willingly adapted to their new conditions.

Finally Carlson broke the unit into groups of three, calling them fire groups. The private first class led the group and each man was equipped with Thompson machine guns and a Browning automatic rifle (BAR). The captain led his platoon with two rifle companies, each equipped with new M1 rifles. The weapons platoon carried lightweight mortars and machine guns. All weapons needed to be carried by only one man, with the exception of the machine gun team. Each member of the gun team carried either a machine gun or the gun's base while a third man carried the ammunition.

Roosevelt approved the plan with Carlson in command and James Roosevelt as the executive officer. Major James Roosevelt had just been transferred over to Carlson's new Marine Raiders. The upper echelon of the Marine Corps hierarchy did not like the new plan. Why should they change? The marines had always operated as an amphibious force, to take the beach and then secure it for the Army. They were not pleased when the orders came down from the commander-in-chief that an upstart and the president's son would command a battalion, an elite one at that.

After Carlson and Roosevelt screened the over 7,000 applicants for the 2nd Marine Raiders they selected only 1,000 men they thought qualified. Of those men, Ray Bauml and an 18-year-old Iowa boy named Bud Nodland were chosen as Marine Raiders.

The selected men trained harder than they had in boot camp. The 2nd Marines used a place just outside of San Diego called Jack's Farm. From there they trained, disembarking off of destroyers in the waters around San Clemente Island in California. They continued to train on the island's terrain in mock combat against each other.

From California, the 2nd Marine Raiders, Carlson's Raiders were transported to Hawaii for extensive training for Pacific Island warfare training. They saw no action during the Battle of Midway and were brought back to Hawaii for even more training.

Then in August 1941, Carlson, Roosevelt, and 120 men boarded two submarines for a surprise attack on the Japanese on the little Pacific atoll known as Makin Island.

The concept of using a submarine to carry troops was brilliant and had it not been for an accidental weapon's discharge, the surprise against the Japanese garrison on the island would have been complete. After a brief but intense two-day fight, Carlson and his troops emerged victorious with the loss of 19 men. What he and his raiders accomplished gave America an incredible morale boost. The sole mission of this raid was to divert Japanese attention from the invasion force landing on the beaches of Guadalcanal. They were also responsible for interrupting communications and the destruction of fuel and ammunition on the island.

During the Makin Island fight, James Roosevelt risked his life on numerous occasions and thus became a Navy Cross recipient. His citation can be read in its entirety at the *Military Times* website.

Roosevelt had proved that he was not a "desk marine." After fighting their way back to the beaches and an incredible fight against ocean waves and currents, Carlson and most of his men paddled their way back to the submarines from which they were off-loaded. Ray Bauml remembered seeing Major "Jimmy" Roosevelt wearing black, high-top tennis shoes. He was the only person in the U.S. Marine Corps authorized to wear them. His flat feet wouldn't allow him to wear combat boots.

The journey back to Hawaii meant another nine days travel on the navy submarines.

Carlson, Roosevelt, and their raiders arrived in Pearl Harbor to a hero's welcome. All the men felt a huge sense of loss for their fallen marine brothers.

On September 4, Colonel Carlson delivered a moving eulogy for the men who were killed on Makin Island. In attendance were Admiral Chester Nimitz, the Marine Raiders, and sailors from the two submarines the *Argonaut* and the *Nautilus* as were other dignitaries.

> We are gathered here today to honor the memory of our comrades who remain at Makin. We miss them. Each had his special place among us, and that place is imperishably his. Being human, we mourn the loss of each. But I believe that these gallant men who so eagerly, so willingly went forth to meet the enemy would not have us weep and bemoan their passing . . . (To read the entire eulogy visit http://www.usmarineraiders.org/makin.html)

On September 6, 1942, Carlson's Raiders left Camp Catlin and headed by troop transport to the New Hebrides Islands to Espirito Santo, located about 500 miles south of Guadalcanal in the Solomon Islands. It took 16 days to slip beneath the Southern Cross. The raiders would stay there until November.

While in route, Carlson began writing letters to the next of kin of all those killed or lost on Makin. In a letter dated September 9, 1942, he wrote:

Mrs. Carolyn Nodland
212 South Center Street,
Marshalltown, Iowa.

Dear Mrs. Nodland:

On behalf of myself, and of the officers and men of this organisation [*sic*], I wish to express the deepest sympathy in the loss of your son, Franklin M. Nodland, who was killed at Makin on August 17.

Franklin was with the advance elements of this command when he met the enemy. His death was instantaneous, and he suffered no pain.

He was a grand youngster, loved and respected by his comrades. He went into this conflict knowing that only through determination and self-sacrifice can we hope to defeat the enemy, retain our freedom and bring peace to our shores. In the battle he was vigorous and courageous. It was his spirit and spirit of others like him that gave us the victory.

Words cannot compensate for his loss, but please know that he died like a man and a patriot. All of us join with you in mourning his loss.

Sincerely,
Evans F. Carlson
Lieutenant Colonel, USMCR
Commanding

Bud was killed eight months after joining the Marine Corps. He never returned to Iowa during that time and never celebrated another Christmas with his family. The holiday would never be the same in the Nodland household.

Once on New Hebrides, the memories of their fallen friends weighed heavy on the minds of Carlson's Raiders. While there, someone carved out a plaque with all of the men's names and their hometowns. It was placed on the outskirts of the camp.

After the raiders departed New Hebrides by transport, they never returned to the island, and the fate of their plaque remains unknown.

While in the New Hebrides, Major James Roosevelt was promoted to lieutenant colonel and he was given command of the 4th Marine Raider Battalion.

Carlson and his Raiders landed on Guadalcanal on November 4 without incident. General Vandergrift ordered Carlson to make his way inland from the beach to Henderson Field. His job was to destroy the Japanese positions.

Remembering his experiences in Nicaragua and China, Carlson used his knowledge of guerilla warfare to great advantage.

Ray Bauml remembered Carlson used the main body of the raiders as an enveloping force. They would strike the Japanese at right angles and fade off back into the bush. He used this tactic again and again with great results. He also remembered the death of Lieutenant Jack Miller. Ray was right next to Miller when a sniper killed him. Ray had taken cover behind an ironwood tree about the same time Miller was shot. That tree saved Ray Bauml's life. Miller died of head wounds shortly thereafter. Because his death came in a forward area, he was buried on the side of the trail. His body was never recovered.

Ray also remembered that the raiders continued their practice of the three-man fire teams. Carlson felt that if his Raiders maintained constant contact, he could make the Japanese feel though an enemy attack was imminent. Carlson's Raiders always moved separately and fluidly. They would then vanish back into the bush to pick their time and place to attack.

Ray recalled how often Carlson deliberately assembled all his uncommitted troops, weapons, and supplies at a point well off the trails but always near the enemy flank. After letting his men rest, Carlson's well-planned, fully supported assault, hit the Japanese when they least expected it.

Carlson employed native guides, who were incredibly helpful with their knowledge of the terrain and their ability to move undetected in the bush.

The raiders also never exposed their base of operations. Carlson constantly moved it. Ray later remembered, "The Japs never did quite figure out what old man was doing. The Japanese showed a steady decrease in resistance."

"Guadalcanal was miserable." Ray explained, "We were wet all of the time, either from sweat or rain. In our patrols, we crossed numerous streams and rivers and climbed a steep ridgeline dividing the Lunga and Tenaru valleys using the ropes we carried." He also remembered that humanity rarely accompanies emotion in the heat of battle.

"Almost everyone had jungle rot on their crotches and legs so bad that that we often stopped to empty the blood out of our boots"; and went on to say, "It was common to find live worms in your own feces as you went to the bathroom" (Bauml, 2000–2010).

After having spent a month in the jungle, Carlson and his 2nd Marine Raiders advanced over 150 miles, killing 700 Japanese soldiers and wounding many more. Carlson's losses were 17 killed and 17 wounded.

When the long march ended for the raiders, they were given a brief respite and then ordered to Bougainville in the Solomon Islands. Of all the places, Ray Bauml fought in, "Bougainville was the most miserable. . . . I had my hammock with me and tied it off between two palm trees every chance I had . . . if I hadn't done that I would have been laying in a constant layer of water and mud."

Guadalcanal was lush, but much of Bougainville's terrain was triple canopy (three layers) of jungle.

Carlson and Roosevelt soon learned that after the Battle in Bougainville ended, the Marine Raiders would be disbanded.

According to Ray, the raiders were getting too many favorable reviews from the press; and Hollywood was even calling to make a film about their exploits. The Marine Corps generals were jealous.

The Marine Corps terminated the raiders' organization in 1943 and the new battalion commander, who replaced Carlson, returned to the standard of a 10-man Marine squad while abolishing concept of the rifle squad with three "fire teams." All the raiders were incorporated into standard Marine Corps units.

That same year, Carlson was sent to the island of Tarawa in the South Pacific as an observer. Throughout the action he voluntarily carried vital information through enemy fire back and forth from the frontlines to the division headquarters.

In 1944, during the Battle for Saipan, Carlson was wounded by enemy fire, during an attempt to rescue an injured Marine on the front line observation post. Carlson's wounds forced his evacuation back to the United States, and caused his retirement from the Marine Corps. Upon retirement he was advanced to brigadier general. He lived his remaining years in Brightwood, Oregon. On May 27, 1947, at the age of 51, Evans F. Carlson passed away of heart disease. He was buried with full military honors at Arlington National Cemetery in Arlington, Virginia.

In 1943, Colonel James Roosevelt arrived home to the United States. In October 1945, following five years of active service, he was transferred to inactive duty.

He annually participated in periods of active duty with the Marine Corps Reserve until he retired on October 1, 1959. Upon retirement, Roosevelt was promoted to brigadier general for his combat citation. In November 1954, he was elected U.S. representative to the 84th Congress. He served as congressman from California from the 84th through the 89th Congresses.

James Roosevelt passed away on August 13, 1991, from complications of a stroke and Parkinson's disease. His death was four days short of marking the 50th anniversary of the Makin Island raid of August 17, 1942. He was buried in Pacific View Memorial Park in Corona del Mar, Orange County, California.

Story Notes

I had never heard much about James Roosevelt or Evans Carlson. My information about Marine Raiders was sketchy at best until I met my friend Ray Bauml almost eight years ago. He is an incredible oral historian who told me about the actions in which he participated in the South Pacific. He personally knew Carlson and Roosevelt and to this day holds in undying love and respect for these two incredible men, as do all who served with them.

After the war, during Raider reunions, Roosevelt was always completely approachable to his men.

Chapter 13

From the Navy Hymn to Davy Jones' Locker: Gordon Skinner

Volumes have been written on the tactics and ship's commanders in WWII navy warfare but little can be found about the everyday sailor. In this chapter we follow the navy career of one such seaman, from boot camp to the end of the war.

Note: This story contains some navy terminology that may not be familiar to some readers. Check the glossary at the end of the story for meanings.

You might say the military was in Gordon Skinner's blood. Ever since the War of 1812, a member of Gordon Skinner's family had served in the military in all of America's wars up to WWII. And although no one in his family served in Korea, his son Lee Skinner served on the rivers of Vietnam in the U.S. Navy.

Growing up with this family history, it seemed Gordon was destined to serve in the military; but in the fall of 1939, it was the last thing on his mind. Anderson, Indiana, a small industrial town located 40 miles northeast of Indianapolis suffered the Depression like cities and towns across American; but Gordon's family was fortunate in that his father, a fireman, was never without work.

At 15 years of age, Gordon was still attending high school and working as much as he could in as many places as he could to help the family. He was employed by the Burt T. Owens Dairy and the Indiana Ice and Dairy Company, where he worked as an assistant to a deliveryman, Arnold Ward, whom Gordon called Benedict (Arnold). Ward was not an easy man to get along with and being called Benedict Arnold by a teenage boy didn't help his disposition. Ward fired Gordon at least once a week, because the young man wasn't afraid of his boss's temper. But early the next morning, Ward would always wake Gordon up and ask him to come back, because Gordon could do the job.

Yes, Gordon Skinner was what people in his day called a hellion. At 16, Gordon fought at the drop of a hat—and a majority of the time he didn't need the hat.

Once a drunk driver sideswiped the milk truck. Words flew, and so did Arnold when the drunk got out of his car to "whip his butt." The drunk, a huge man, then tried to climb onto the step of the slow moving milk truck to get at Gordon. As the man stepped up to get into the truck, Gordon slammed on the breaks, which sent the drunk flying over the hood of the truck. Gordon then jumped out with an empty milk bottle and told the man he would use it if he didn't follow him down to the police department to report the accident. Tired and beaten, the man did so without an argument.

"Things were just so different back then." Gordon later recalled.

Even as a teen, Gordon proved to be resourceful. Three years earlier, in 1936, Gordon's father ran into a situation in which Gordon could purchase his first car. Because of the hard times, a farmer ran up a $25 bill in the local feed store and couldn't pay it back. The man did have a 1929 model A Ford, so the store took it. With money from his savings Gordon was able to purchase the vehicle for $25! Later he was able to upgrade to a 1933 Ford V-8. It needed work, including a head gasket, but Gordon's uncle Otto taught him the fundamentals of engine repair. This vehicle gave Gordon the kind of freedom and speed he had never known before and soon began exploring the countryside and nearby towns.

Still, in 1939, Gordon wasn't thinking much about his future. In the fall of 1940, Gordon met a second cousin, a retired navy chief named "Mac" McCarty, who had been visiting family and friends. Mac had been a "China sailor" and was a WWI and submarine veteran. Gordon later remembered that he had a nose "that was over on one side of his face." And the spirited teen loved hearing the old salt's stories.

Mac was a sailor's sailor. He thrilled Gordon with tales of his adventures in exotic ports of call in places all over the world. The two became close friends and stayed in touch until a few years later when Mac succumbed to throat cancer. After hearing Mac's stories, Gordon was determined to go to sea. And on January 29, 1941, at age 17, Gordon Skinner enlisted in the U.S. Navy. Because he was underage, his mother had to sign a permission slip.

Boot Camp

Gordon was sent to the Great Lakes Naval Training Center in Great Lakes, Illinois. Like the other navy recruits, he marched and did various forms of physical training almost constantly. And he learned the fundamentals of seamanship. The recruits were issued a sea bag, a laundry bag, and a "ditty bag." The ditty bag was a small white canvas bag in which toiletries were kept and it was packed into the larger sea bag. When folded right, all uniforms, underwear, and toiletries would fit perfectly into this white canvas carry all. All recruits were also issued the Navy's official bible, the *Blue Jacket's Manual*. Everything anyone needed to know about the Navy, from its history and regulations to tying every knot ever known and nautical terms could be found in this book. The manual helped the recruit transition from civilian life into navy life, by clearly explaining what would happen from the day they arrived to what would happen when they graduated. They were taught the chain of command and their position in it; at the top of that chain were the chief **petty officers**.

Any recruit or seaman who did something against the chief's orders or the laws of the universe, was greeted with screams of, "Did your mother have any kids that lived?" or "Don't take this personally maggot, but you are one ugly human being!"

These navy veterans sported "hash marks" on their dress uniforms. Each diagonal stripe on the lower half of the left sleeve stood for four years of service. One old chief boatswain mate had 11 gold hash marks on his uniforms, which meant he had been in the Navy for a minimum of 44 years! He had been a South China Sea sailor during the Boxer Rebellion of 1900. The "old boats" (bosun mates) said that he'd been in the Navy for so long that he remembered, "When the Good Lord was only a seaman recruit . . . that was before He knew how to walk on water." And that he was so old, he could remember, "When the Dead Sea was only sick."

In boot camp, the most experienced navy veterans trained the recruits. Their language was salty, and their message sometimes punctuated with physical punishment. If one man in a company made a flagrant mistake, all 80 men would be punished. Push-ups were common penalties, as were slaps up along the back of the head or being required to run with a rifle held high above the head for a distance. And if a recruit talked back in a disrespectful way, he could expect to be punched in the mouth or between the eyes. Gordon was lucky though. His company commander, Chief Goldfarb used a totally different approach to the recruits in his charge. There was no physical abuse, but Chief Goldfarb could humiliate his company if they didn't perform when he knew they could.

January in the Great Lakes boot camp was cold. Gordon and his company often spent the coldest of days in the barracks learning how to tie knots that were essential to life aboard ship.

Another boot camp basic was heard every Sunday with the official navy hymn, "Eternal Father" a prayer "for those in peril on the sea."

Aboard the USS *Yorktown*

After graduating boot camp, Gordon received orders to proceed to the aircraft carrier USS *Yorktown* (CV-5). The ship's homeport was Norfolk, Virginia. On the day he turned 18, Gordon was sent out on patrol in the Atlantic Ocean.

He later remembered thinking, "I joined the Navy to see the sea and what did I see? The sea."

By December 1941, Gordon Skinner was promoted to third class electrician's mate. Gordon was aboard ship, which was moored in her homeport in Norfolk, Virginia on December 7 when the word was passed about the Japanese attack on Pearl Harbor. Amidst the chaos in the city streets, Gordon and his friend Pete Newberg decided to go into the city because, as Gordon later recalled, "We just didn't know when we'd get ashore again."

What they found was a city in shock and turmoil. In downtown Norfolk, Gordon and Pete saw two Asian men with signs around their necks that read, "We are Chinese," hoping not to be confused with Japanese citizens, thus saving them from a beating or more serious bodily injuries.

Back on the *Yorktown*, all preparations for war were being made. The ship immediately went in for a complete overhaul. To his amazement, Gordon and the *Yorktown*'s crew were spared from all hands hanging off the sides of the ship scraping and repainting her, because the *Yorktown* went into dry dock. For expediency's sake, she was sand blasted, painted, and made ready for her journey to the Pacific. Gordon never doubted that America would handle this war quickly and at the same time, was terrified that the war would be over before he got there. He had no idea what the next four years would bring.

En Route to War

The *Yorktown* finally departed Norfolk, and made her way down and through the Panama Canal. When the crew was granted liberty, Gordon and many of his friends headed for the seediest part of Panama to celebrate and have fun. But their misdeeds and adventures were short lived, and all hands soon reported back to the ship.

Shortly thereafter, liberties were cancelled altogether; and the *Yorktown* resumed her journey through the Panama Canal. The passage in itself was an adventure, in that the locks in the canal were only 110 feet wide and the *Yorktown*'s hull was 108 feet. There was only one foot of clearance on both port and starboard sides! The flight deck overlooked the land on either side of the canal.

After this harrowing feat of navigation through the locks, the *Yorktown* proceeded north in the Pacific to San Diego. She arrived on December 30, exactly three weeks and two days after the bombing of Pearl Harbor. Her orders were to join two cruisers and four destroyers and escort the Matson luxury ocean liners, the *Lurline*, the *Monterey*, and the *Matsonia* to Samoa. Also included in this **convoy** were the USS *Jupiter* and USS *Lassen*, two cargo ships. The three luxury liners each carried over 3,000 marines and all of their equipment. The *Yorktown* was the flagship of the newly formed Task Force 17.

The *Yorktown* and Task Force 17 arrived in Samoa on January 20, 1942, and then departed for Pearl Harbor. In a brief detour near the Gilbert Islands, the

Yorktown participated in their first skirmish with the Japanese—this time without casualties. Then she proceeded to Pearl Harbor, reaching there on February 7. Entering the harbor, Gordon, the men of the *Yorktown*, and the rest of the task force stood amazed at what they saw. "We were **standing quarters** on the flight deck when entering the harbor," Gordon recalls. "We couldn't believe the amount of people on shore giving us three cheers. It was like the entire population had turned out" (Skinner, 2004).

The people of Hawaii had been living in fear of an invasion; and the sight of this task force brought incredible comfort and reassurance. The people of the islands could now see that their country's armed forces were still intact.

Battle of the Coral Sea

Within days, shipboard boredom turned to sheer terror when the *Yorktown* was ordered to proceed toward the Solomon Islands. It was near here that the U.S. Navy engaged the Imperial Japanese Navy in the Battle of Coral Sea, northeast of Australia, in the first major naval engagement of the war and the first naval battle in history that was fought entirely by aircraft. Although American and Japanese ships never made visual contact with each other, at one point they were only 30 miles apart.

During **general quarters**, Gordon ran all out to his battle station. Rounding a corner in the passageway, "boom!" he ran headlong into Rear Admiral Frank Jack Fletcher, knocking the officer on his butt. This admiral was also a Medal of Honor recipient. So Gordon's first thought was "Portsmouth Naval Prison here I come." But as the admiral got up, he simply looked at Gordon and dismissed him, saying, "Carry on lad." Gordon, acting a little like the comic book character "the Flash," was instantly gone and up to his station on the flight deck.

Chief Machinist Mate Bill Kowalczewski had been on the *Yorktown* since 1940, as had his older brother Victor. For a year and a half, they shared the same duty compartment during general quarter drills below decks in damage control repair five. They always sat side by side.

At 11:27 a.m., on the second day of the Battle of Coral Sea, for reasons Bill doesn't remember, the division officer, Lieutenant Milton Ricketts, called Bill away from the compartment. Bill was ordered out of the compartment and into the passageway. Almost immediately after he left, a Japanese bomb hit the ship, completely destroying the compartment, and instantly killing his brother as well as almost everybody else in it.

The impact of the explosion bounced Bill around the passageway, but he was unharmed. In intense fighting the sailors of the *Yorktown* battled fires above and below decks. Lieutenant Milton Ernest Ricketts, though mortally wounded, deployed a fire hose and successfully contained the resulting fire before he died. He was posthumously awarded the Medal of Honor for heroism.

Not far from where Seaman 1st Pete Montalvo was passing ammunition for one of the 1.1 anti-aircraft guns on the flight deck, a bomb went off and hit the gun mount. The bomb shrapnel cut the gun pointer in half. As Gordon recalls, "Pete's guts were hanging out and he was on fire." Gordon also noticed how close the ammunition was to the gun, and knew it could easily blow up. Grabbing a high-pressure hose, "with almost no pressure while Pete was still holding his guts in" Gordon put the fire out. Gordon's quick actions prevented a disaster (Skinner, 2004).

Gordon and others got Pete to **sick bay,** where the navy doctors and corpsmen worked surgical wonders. It truly was a miracle that Pete survived, not only the Battle of Coral Sea, but he lived well into his senior years.

The *Yorktown* would have been lost had it not been for crew's efficiency in damage control and firefighting. She barely made it back to Pearl Harbor, leaving an oil streak in her wake from the Coral Sea to Hawaii. The only stop along the way was in the island of Tonga Tabu for a quick patch to the hull by navy divers. They were there less than three days. The *Yorktown* then continued on her 3,000-mile oil-streaked journey back to Pearl Harbor.

The carrier *Lexington* was not as lucky. Most of her crew was rescued, but the ship was lost. The U.S. Navy had fought the Japanese to a standstill.

In the Battle of Coral Sea, the U.S. Navy lost one fleet oiler, one aircraft carrier, and one destroyer; and it did major damage to the *Yorktown*. However, because of this battle, the Japanese then aborted their seaborne invasion of Port Moresby. They lost one destroyer, one light carrier, and several small ships. In addition, bombing inflicted serious damage on the *Shokaku* carrier; and almost entirely wiped out the *Zuikaku*'s air group. Both the *Shokaku* and the *Zuikaku* were ultimately handicapped from participating in the upcoming Midway operation.

After finally making it to Pearl Harbor, all liberties were canceled and the repair crews began working around the clock to make the *Yorktown* seaworthy. They completed repairs in 72 hours—a miracle in itself.

Battle of Midway

On June 4, 1942, the Navy again took on the Imperial Japanese Navy in another important battle—the Battle of Midway. This time it was a decisive victory for the United States; but one of the casualties was the mighty *Yorktown*. After having survived the battle and again being severely damaged, a Japanese submarine torpedoed her on June 7.

When the crew received the order to abandon ship, Gordon Skinner gave his life jacket to a man he describes only as "chief quarter," explaining, "I don't remember his first name. He was somewhere in his fifties and not a big man physically. I knew I could swim, but wasn't sure he would survive without it. I just didn't want his death by drowning on my conscience." Meanwhile, the grand old *Yorktown* slipped, bow first, 16,000 feet below the waters of the Pacific, a place commonly called "Davey Jones' Locker." The majority of the crew was soon rescued and sent to Hawaii.

Survivors of the USS *Yorktown* were sequestered near Camp Catlin, a training ground for an elite Marine force called "Carlson's Raiders." *Yorktown* musician, clarinet player Tommy Thompson was sent out to Hawaii's famed cemetery the Punch Bowl, where he spent two weeks digging graves for later use.

Like Tommy, Gordon, and the rest of the *Yorktown*'s crew hung in a sort of limbo. All of their records, including pay, medical, and personnel had gone down with the ship along with their uniforms, sea bags, and personal effects. And worse for Gordon, he was bored to death. He had two weeks of no money and no real change of clothes to go anywhere.

One day, while exploring their surroundings, Gordon Skinner and his friend Pete Newberg found a parked jeep. Gordon, looking at Pete, said, "let's steal that jeep!" "How we gonna steal that jeep without a key?" asked Pete. Intimately acquainted in the ways of hotwiring a car, Gordon grinned and said, "Well Pete, you don't need a key." He hotwired the jeep in less than two minutes and the two then proceeded to go for a joyride.

When their burst of freedom was over the two sailors brought the jeep back. As they pulled in to park the vehicle, Gordon and Pete were approached by what Gordon later described as a "9-foot Marine sergeant" (he gets taller with each telling).

He knew what the two sailors had experienced. He told them firmly, yet politely, that they could not have this jeep. The sergeant then said, "now if you want to steal a jeep, go ahead, but you can't have this one. You see this one belongs to the Major."

Gordon still doesn't know why he asked, but he did, "Major who?"

"Major Roosevelt," came the reply.

"You mean THE ROOSEVELT?" Gordon asked.

All the sergeant did was shake his head yes. Gordon and Pete were too shocked to argue. They had just stolen the jeep of the president of the United States' oldest son, Major James Roosevelt, the executive officer of Carlson's 2nd Marine Raiders (Skinner, 2004).

Aboard the Submarine *Sterlet*

Two weeks later, Gordon, along with most of the *Yorktown*'s black gang (enginemen, firemen, machinist mates, and electrician's mates) were transferred to the USS *West Virginia*. She along with the *California* and the *Nevada* (all are battle ships) had been resurrected and refloated from their Pearl Harbor graves.

Gordon served on the *West Virginia* until late 1943. In May of that year, the *West Virginia* sailed east to Bremerton, Washington, to the Naval Ship

Yard for extensive repairs. While there, Gordon requested to transfer off the *West Virginia*. His request was granted; he was ordered to the Naval Submarine School in New London, Connecticut, and after six weeks of training he graduated.

While stationed in New London, Gordon found incredible kindness in, of all places, the local police department. When granted liberty from the Submarine School during training, he and a couple of his buddies sometimes went into Groton and neighboring Ledyard. Late at night, when they couldn't afford a hotel, they found that the local police would often let them sleep in an empty jail cell. More than that, when the sailors woke up the next day, the police chief always had breakfast waiting for them. Gordon has never forgotten the kindness he found in that small town.

After graduating in early 1944, Gordon was assigned to the USS *Sterlet* (SS-392), a **Balao class** (thick skinned) **submarine**. Thick skinned meant she could dive much deeper than other submarines classified as "thin skinned."

The *Sterlet*'s home port was the desolate island of Midway located in the middle of the Pacific Ocean, not far from where the *Yorktown* had sunk. Her skipper was Captain Hugh Lewis.

The irony of this was that in his new ship, Gordon became one of the silent hunters of the open sea, whereas on the *Yorktown* he had been the hunted, and that ship was a casualty of war.

The remaining 17 months of WWII, the *Sterlet* submarine was triumphant in five more war patrols. Gordon participated in four of those patrols.

"You know, it was incredibly peaceful when cruising underwater" Gordon recalls, "didn't have to worry about rough seas or any noise except shipboard sounds . . . even that would quiet down if you were under **depth charge attacks**. If you didn't have an assigned place during a depth charge attack, the best place to be was your bunk. There would be no talking or extraneous noise," he continued.

Silence was vital because enemy sonar could pick up any manmade sounds. When the depth charge attacks commenced, there was to be no panic, even though the submarine would be violently shaken and men being bounced around. Gordon remembers, "If a depth charge went off within twenty-five feet of the sub . . . you were dead, particularly if it went off below the ship. The pressure would come up and rupture the hull."

The *Sterlet*'s maximum diving depth was recommended at 450 feet, but sometimes the helmsman chose to go deeper, much deeper, and pray that the ship could withstand the pressure. In one incident, a depth charge was dropped from a Japanese plane and the *Sterlet* dived to a depth of 737 feet! It amazed everyone on the ship. And with each attack, the common thought of every man was "when is it going to stop?"

Hysterics and panic were rare, and wouldn't be tolerated. Gordon remembered one officer on the *Sterlet* was praying aloud and with great fervor during an attack. "I think everybody was praying, but we kept it to ourselves" (Skinner, 2004). This officer was transferred off the ship. Praying aloud could have panicked the others.

Unlike Hollywood's ideas about the Submarine Service, most of the *Sterlet*'s patrols were at night with the ship running on the surface. "We could run faster and maneuver much quicker than we could underwater." Gordon explains, "Besides, the Japanese navy didn't have effective surface radar. When underwater, the *Sterlet*'s cruising depth was between 150–200 feet."

Gordon remembers that, "We'd normally follow convoy and got up behind it to pick off tankers, freighters and warships. The main targets were oil tankers. If the enemy had no fuel, then their war efforts couldn't move . . . and convoys were also very slow. They could only travel about 12 knots (one knot equals 1.151 miles per hour)."

Under the constant pressure and fear, humor often eased the tension. In one incident Doyle "Light Lunch" Lester woke up a ship mate during a depth charge attack that was miles off its target. This same man had been without sleep for days. Everyone aboard the *Sterlet* could hear the depth charges going off, but also knew they were miles away. "Light lunch" (called that because he could out eat any man on the ship and never gain weight) woke the sleeping sailor just to let him know they were under attack. It was like telling someone who was in the middle of a blizzard that it was snowing, and everyone had a good laugh.

Petty Officer Jarvis

Life was never dull aboard the *Sterlet*. While out at sea, Petty Officer Jarvis saw another officer fall overboard. In fact, no one really knew if he fell overboard or if he was washed over by a wave, but it didn't matter. There was no discussion— Jarvis just acted on it.

It was night and the seas were rough. Jarvis was about to dive in after the man, but because of the danger, had to be restrained. He then got a long piece of line (rope) and tied it around his waist. Without hesitation, he dived in the darkness. Somehow he found the officer and was able to save his life. Everyone on the *Sterlet* knew this was the kind of man Jarvis was; he was popular with both enlisted men and officers.

Later, off the coast of Japan, Jarvis lost his temper at an **ensign** who had a tendency to treat all enlisted men badly. Jarvis got so mad he had to be physically held back by other crewmembers from punching that officer. As a result, the ensign put Jarvis on report and he was made to stand a captain's mast, the lowest form of courts-martial (a military trial).

At the end of Jarvis's captain's mast, Captain Lewis said, "Jarvis, I am going to make an example of you. I am cancelling your shore leave." Of course, they were a thousand miles from any place they could have had any shore leave. Captain Lewis also made sure that the ensign was reassigned as soon as this particular war patrol was over. In his report, Captain Lewis said, "This man should have no contact with any enlisted men whatsoever and be confined to shore duty. He is not fit to go out to sea" (Skinner, 2004).

The *Sterlet*'s Legacy

The *Sterlet*'s war record was incredible. During the short time she served in WWII, she sank more than 10 Japanese ships totaling 54,900 tons. She damaged a 5,000-ton vessel, rescued eight allied pilots, and managed to take only one prisoner of war. All these efforts awarded her officers and crew 33 decorations including the submarine insignia with four golden stars.

In the last month of the war, Gordon participated in a patrol that took the *Sterlet* in and around the waters of Tinian Island. At the time, he and the rest of the crew had no idea that they were a part of a protective patrol of the island. However, as it turned out, the *Enola Gay*, a B-29 was based on Tinian awaiting her flight over Japan on August 6, 1945, to drop the first atomic bomb in history on the city of Hiroshima. That bomb and the second one dropped over Nagasaki changed the history of warfare. In fact, nuclear power as a source of limitless energy changed life not only for the military but also for the civilians. Power plants, medical research, and treatment revolutionized the 20th century

Almost all the submarines of WWII were powered by diesel, only a few used gas. The submarines' batteries only allowed them enough power to stay submerged for 20 hours. That changed on January 17, 1955, when Commander William R. Anderson, the first commanding officer of the USS *Nautilus* ordered, "All lines cast off" and signaled the memorable and historic message, "Underway on Nuclear Power." Today, all of America's submarines are nuclear powered, capable of circumnavigating the earth underwater without ever having to surface to recharge batteries.

Gordon Skinner remained in the Navy until 1946, and was honorably discharged. During his navy career, he had watched the U.S. Navy evolve from a "battleship navy" to an "aircraft carrier navy." The battleship, once the mightiest ship ever to sail, had become obsolete on the morning of December 7, 1941, when the Pacific fleets' battleships were all sunk at Pearl Harbor. Gordon also witnessed the growth and importance of aircraft carriers and watched as the submarine sails her way into the modern navy and becomes one of this nation's first lines of defense.

Glossary

Balao class submarine: An improved class of WWII submarine that allowed the ship to dive at deeper depths. Its hull was designed to withstand the tremendous pressure of very deep submersions of the ship.

Convoy: Ships traveling together escorted by warships.

Depth charge attacks: A depth charge is basically an underwater bomb set to go off at certain depths to sink submarines.

Ensign: Equivalent to a 2nd Lieutenant (the lowest and junior ranks of officers).

General quarters: "Battle stations." All officers and crewmen are assigned certain tasks throughout the ship for maximum efficiency during battle. Everyone is trained in seamanship, firefighting, and watertight integrity (making all compartments watertight to avoid flooding).

Petty officer: Equivalent to a corporal up through sergeants, that is, a navy third-class petty officer is the same rank as an army corporal.

Sick bay: The ship's hospital or dispensary.

Standing quarters: Whenever a ship arrives or leaves port, all hands line up either on the port (left side) or starboard (right side) of the ship in dress uniforms as a show of manpower on the ship. This has been a navy tradition for over a hundred years.

Story Notes

I have been fortunate to have Gordon Skinner in my life. I met him years ago at a reunion of the USS Yorktown. We became friends and he has opened up and shared the incredible stories of his life in the U.S. Navy. Gordon and I try to talk on the telephone at least once a week. Our conversations last at least an hour. Like I said, I have been fortunate in having this hero in my life. He is part of what newsman Tom Brokaw has called "The Greatest Generation."

Gordon Skinner's story is unique in the history of navy. He was among a very few sailors who witnessed and survived WWII aboard two very different fighting ships, an aircraft carrier and a submarine. The dates and actions in this story are from Gordon Skinner's personal memories.

Chapter 14

In the Shadow of Giants:
Ray Bauml

*Before there were U.S. Army Rangers, Green Berets, or Navy SEALs,
there was an elite U.S. Marine Corps group known as Carlson's Raiders.
Their story was born in the very early months of WWII. This is one man's
experiences of that time in America's first land victory over the Japanese in
August 1942.*

Before the War

In the fall of 1939, just a few miles from the shores of Lake Michigan, Ray
Bauml attended Morton Jr. College in Cicero, Illinois, a suburb of Chicago. A
football star and a letterman, he was only seven months away from graduation.
He was witty, humorous, and known as a "master of words" for his command
of the English language by those who knew him. He was also a master on the
dance floor in that era of swing. It was here in Cicero, on a November day, that
he met Lillian Vosicky. A mutual friend on campus had introduced them.

She was pretty, gentle, and quiet, and somewhat introverted. But Lillian
was quick to smile and laugh, and Ray made her do both.

On their first date they went to see Judy Garland in *The Wizard of Oz*. They
walked a half mile to the movie theater, hoping to get there in time for the 15-cent
show. After 6:00 p.m. the price went up to a quarter. When they got there, Ray had to
borrow 20 cents from Lil to have enough money to purchase the tickets.

For Ray and Lil, the movie was pure enchantment. They, as audiences
throughout America, were transported through a visual realm of L. Frank Baum's
classic books, and were captivated by Judy Garland's singing of "Somewhere
over the Rainbow." As Lil remembered, "it became our song."

This chapter is based on a one-on-one interview conducted with Mr. Ray Bauml. Direct quotes
are used throughout the entire chapter.

But on the other side of the Atlantic, there were no rainbows. And it was becoming increasingly apparent that something more horrifying than the "Wicked Witch of the West" and her flying monkeys had descended from the clouds of Europe. After "annexing" Austria, the German dictator, Adolph Hitler invaded Czechoslovakia and then Poland. England declared war on Germany, 1939. Later developments in these countries had a profound effect on many of this country's immigrants in the States—Ray Bauml's grandparents were from Czechoslovakia, as were Lillian's parents.

Lil's father and uncle owned a tailor shop, Vosicky Brothers, just around the corner from the Lexington Hotel, home to Al Capone. Many of Capone's men did business with the Vosicky Brothers, as their work was first class. Lillian learned to sew from her father; and she worked part-time at the shop. In this era, Cicero was the safest place in the Chicago area; there being an agreement with all of the urban gangs that there would be no violence in this suburb. Even the local hoodlums kept their acts clean for fear of Capone's retribution.

During the school years of 1938–1940, Ray Bauml held a part-time job, washing windows at the local high school. He also worked what other odd jobs he could find, no matter how menial. In the summers, he worked in the farm fields of Anamosa, Iowa. The hours were long, and there was no money. Ray worked for room and board only to help lighten the living expenses of his parents.

In the spring of 1939, half way around the world, the Pacific Island of Butaritari was still paradise to its island people. They did not suffer from the ills of the so-called civilized world. There was no such thing as crime or violence and there were no unwanted children.

In the spring of 1939, the island of Butaritari was still paradise to the South Sea sailors who dropped anchor here. They called this place the "island of laughter" because the native Polynesians were known for their hospitality and their sense of humor. Their white beaches, below the hundreds of coconut palm trees, were pristine, as were the crystal clear waters above the reefs that surrounded the island.

Within the next two years, their world would change, though. Gone would be the carefree life the Butaritari people had known for hundreds of years. And the sailing ships and sailors. They too would vanish with the coming of the Japanese invasion of these islands and other islands of the South Pacific in December 1941.

Spring in the southern hemisphere is, of course, autumn above the equator; and in that fall of 1939, America was just emerging from the Great Depression. The government had borrowed and spent a billion dollars to build up its armed forces. There was a rumor of war, but most Americans didn't want to hear about it. A war would mean even more hardships and sacrifices; and the memories of WWI and the Great Depression were still too fresh in the American psyche.

Besides, the Big Band era had just arrived a few years earlier. And people were beginning to work and laugh again.

As Ray remembers it, "The financial condition of the area was not that great, and just to get a job was something." So after graduation, in the spring of 1940, Ray worked at Montgomery Wards changing fashions on the mannequins that adorned their windows. Within a year though, Ray found other work with Chicago, Burlington and Quincy Railroad as an office boy. And a short time later he was promoted to a buyer.

Meanwhile, news of Europe and Asia filled the newspapers and radio broadcasts. None of the reports were good. Ray felt this would be a great time to further his "real life" education and career, so he decided to enlist in the Navy in early September. He wanted to be a flyer pilot. He went to the navy recruiters and passed all of his tests, but found that he lacked one requirement— trigonometry. To master this, Ray began classes in night school, but then a real bombshell hit. Ray recalls that in mid-September 1941, while returning from work, he

Was on the "L" hanging from a strap when I noticed my name in the Chicago Tribune another man was reading. Much to my surprise I was at the top of the list of all of the men who had just been drafted.

He received his official induction notice in the mail that same day. Ray was the first person from Oak Park, Illinois, to be drafted.

The Army now wanted Ray; he was expected to report for duty on September 26, 1941. Had he been given the opportunity to finish his trigonometry classes, Ray would have become a navy pilot. He went to the draft board and said, "look gentlemen, in two more weeks I will be in the Navy Air Corps."

But their reaction was typical, "Oh no we can't allow that. We need men like you to fight in the Army."

To Ray, all that meant was numbers. He later said, "For some reason the stigma of being drafted really bothered me, so I joined the Marine Corps." So, the marines promptly sent him off to their boot camp in San Diego, California. After seven weeks of intense training and marching, Ray remembers, "I started out wanting the glamorous life of a Navy flyer and ended up picking up cigarette butts for the Marines."

Marine Corps Boot Camp

In the Marine Corps, the most experienced veterans trained the recruits in boot camp. Their language was salty, and their message was sometimes punctuated with physical punishment. If one man in a company screwed up, all 80 men would be punished. Push-ups, sometimes called the "dead cockroach," were common, as were slaps up along the back of the head. And in many cases, if a recruit talked back, he was punched in the mouth or between the eyes.

Ray remembers one occasion, when the recruit standing next to him was punched square on the nose for a minor infraction. "His nose wasn't broken, but God, there was blood everywhere."

One Philadelphia recruit became the company "guide arm bearer." While guiding his company in pass and review, the drill master on the podium looked down at him and yelled down, "Guide arm bearer, straighten that guide arm up."

The Philadelphia tough guy looked up at him and retorted, "What do you want for two cents an hour?" The whole company paid for that remark. They ran with their rifles held over their heads until they dropped with exhaustion. Needless to say, there were no more comments to any of the drill instructors other than "Sir, Yes Sir!"

A recruit was no longer an individual; he was now a serial number, a "maggot," "mothball," "puke," "scab." Though the term wasn't used in boot camp, the recruit was now—GI—"government issue." A standard saying by sergeants was "Your soul may belong to God, but your butt belongs to me."

A recruit needed permission to do anything that he wasn't ordered to do. If the GI was sent off by their drill instructor on an errand, he would have to "double time" his way across the base, which meant to move very quickly without worrying about marching, while maintaining all military courtesies. The same was true for two men; three or more men would have to march in formation.

If a marine wanted to get married after boot camp, he needed to obtain permission from the Corps. His request was often met with, "If the Marine Corps wanted you to have a wife, they would have issued you one."

A running joke in the Marine Corps lists the five most dangerous things you might hear in the Corps:

> A private saying "I learned this in boot camp,"
> A corporal saying, Trust me, sir."
> A 2nd Lieutenant saying, " based on my experience."
> A 1st Lieutenant saying "I was just thinking."
> And a **Gunny** Sergeant chuckling, "Watch this."

Shortly after 1:00 p.m. on December 7, 1941, as Lillian Vosicky and one of her girlfriends were sitting in a darkened movie theater in Cicero, Illinois, the manager interrupted the movie with the news of the Japanese attack on Pearl Harbor, Hawaii. The rumor of war turned to a bloody reality for Lillian. Her first and only thoughts though were of Ray, and what would happen to him.

As the news came in, Lillian and the rest of the country listened to reports that the battleship *Arizona* was sent to the bottom of the harbor along with 1,100 of its crew. The USS *Utah* was also sunk, and the USS *Oklahoma* was so severely damaged that it would not ever see action. The other six battleships, though heavily damaged, moored there that day would survive.

Hickam Air Field and Schofield barracks were also shot up. Few planes made it into the air. One hundred fifty-one U.S. planes were destroyed on the airfield. Civilians in the area also became victims of this attack. The combination attacks on the fleet, Schofield Army Barracks, the Naval Air Station, and civilian life was devastating. The Naval Air Station, Ford Island, the Pearl Harbor Naval Base and "Battleship Row" on the island of Oahu in the Hawaiian Islands were also attached by the Japanese. The Pacific fleet was in shambles. Over 2,400 people had been killed and 1,200 severely injured.

As for Ray, he was no longer picking up cigarette butts for the Marine Corps. His company had been put on full alert. In the afternoon and evening hours of December 7, he and the others of his company were sent to the California beaches to patrol the shores for the invasion that didn't come. Each man had been given a 1903 Springfield rifle with just one bullet.

Carlson's Raiders

While awaiting orders, Ray was informed that San Diego would become home for the newly formed 2nd Marine Raiders under the command of Lieutenant Colonel Evans Carlson. Carlson now called for volunteers within the Marine Corps for an elite raiding force. Over 7,000 applied, but only 1,000 were chosen. The process of elimination was unique. Besides being physically fit the Raider needed to grasp the political meaning of the war. Their type of warfare would be without quarter.

Ray Bauml was among the first 50 men to be accepted.

Ray remembered that in "all of March and April, 1942 we trained at a place called 'Jack's Farm' just outside San Diego."

And train we did. We were on the go from morning to night; and in fact, we were on the go many, many evenings—throughout the entire night. We did quite a bit of our own cooking, slept on the ground in those little pup tents, walked several miles on maneuvers, at the firing ranges, practiced with and became acquainted with each other's weapon. You name it, we did it. We were becoming Gung-Ho in our attitude. "Gung Ho" was an expression that Colonel Carlson got from the Chinese that means, "Work together."

The small farmhouse was used as battalion headquarters. Directly behind the house was a small barn with a loading platform attached. This platform was used on more than one occasion as we held our Gung-Ho sessions there. These affairs consisted of Colonel Carlson speaking to the raiders about our progress, his experiences in

China, and how they applied to our training. Other times, some of the more talented raiders would perform, such as sing to the group; others would do a skit; and on one occasion, I recall a poem written and recited by Bob Allard. The poem was about our battalion and he received quite an ovation when he finished. After each Gung-Ho session, we sang the Marine Corps Hymn, and the Colonel would ask, in a loud voice, "what do we do when the going gets tough?" The total battalion would respond with "we Gung Ho!" At one of our sessions we had a famous guest. Mrs. Eleanor Roosevelt, wife of the President and mother of the executive officer, Major James Roosevelt, was present and gave us a bit of a speech. She was quite a lady. The battalion serenaded her with the Marine Corps hymn.

Occasional weekend liberties were taken in San Diego, giving the men time off from the intense training. Ray and the others always tried to stay at the Young Man's Christian Association (YMCA) because the rooms were very clean and inexpensive for service men. Living high on the hog meant that if you were lucky enough to get a semiprivate room, it would only cost about 75 cents. It was as close as any of them came to privacy. The men played as hard as they trained. Ray's best friend was Glenn Lincoln who was from Montana. Ray, Glenn, and Ruben Hedger went everywhere together. Hedger was a powerful man who was on Ray's fire team. They also spent time with Bud Nodland, though Ray remembers him as somewhat introvert. He was the third member of Ray's fire team.

After intensive training at Jack's Farm, the 2nd Marine Raiders, Carlson's Raiders were transported to San Clemente Island for rubber boat training in the last days of April and into the first two weeks of May. As Ray remembered,

At first we were quite awkward and incompetent in handling these ungodly rubber boats, eight men learning how to paddle in unison. No motors were used at this time. It really didn't take too long and we became quite adept, even when lowering the boats from the deck of the destroyers. A good part of our time was also spent on the island, Company A in mock combat with Company B. Actually, we rather enjoyed roaming all over the island.

Shipboard life was far different from what Ray and Carlson's Raiders had experienced on land. Time passed slowly; everyday routines became tedious and boring. Rumors ran rampant, and stories abounded about people, places, and events.

During the last two weeks of May, Carlson's Raiders returned to San Diego, as Ray recalled, "we geared up and shipped out to Hawaii. Our camp was situated, roughly about halfway between Pearl Harbor and Honolulu. Camp Catlin, a temporary setup, used by the Marines during the war. Today it is a golf course."

The raiders' time in Hawaii was spent in training, training, and more training, with one major interruption: the Battle of Midway.

To defend Midway Island in case of a Japanese breakthrough, Carlson's 2nd Marine Raiders were sent to the island by destroyers. Ray later described the trip as

> A wild ride . . . the seas were choppy and the **tin cans** were moving all out. Man, were we all sick! Everybody was lying down on the deck; all and everybody was throwing up. We were being drenched with sea spray and vomit . . . what a happy situation . . . We got to Midway, but not for the full battle. We had a few Jap planes fly over though.

Midway was made up of two islands, Eastern and Sand. Sand is where the airstrip was. On that island, Ray found a cairn that proclaimed that Captain Cook had landed there in his second voyage around the world. There were even names on the wood part of the cairn; Ray says he was afraid to touch it because it was so old. At this time in history though, it was not Captain Cook on the island. It was the Imperial Japanese Navy. There were no sails or discoveries now, it was a fleet bent on the total conquest of the Pacific.

Fortunately for the marines, the U.S. Navy defeated the Japanese at Midway. Had they not, superior forces and bombardment from the world's largest battleship, the *Yamato* and her 18-inch guns would have blown the small Islands of Midway and Carlson's Raiders out of existence. Had the Japanese been victorious at Midway, Pearl Harbor and the American West coast would have become vulnerable to attack.

* * *

While Ray Bauml was on Midway, on the other side of the world, the little Czechoslovakian village of Lidice ceased to exist. In the early morning hours of June 10, the German SS forcibly removed all the residents from their homes. By late afternoon, 192 men and boys and 71 women had been executed. They were shot in groups of 10 at a time behind a barn. The other women and most of the children were sent to concentration camps. The SS then leveled the town and tried to eradicate its memory. The name of Lidice was obliterated from all official records. This was all done in retaliation for the assassination of Gestapo leader Reinhard Heydrich only a few days earlier in Prague. He was second only to Heinrich Himmler in the Gestapo hierarchy. In response, Hitler had ordered an entire town's destruction. In addition, he ordered the deaths of another 1,300 innocent Czechs.

Lillian Vosicky's mother was from Lidice. Most of Lillian's immediate family and close friends were killed that day.

* * *

Meanwhile, Ray, Bud Nodland, and their units returned to Pearl Harbor on July 4, 1942. For the next five weeks their training intensified, as did their rubber boat practice at a place they called Salt Lake, and then at Barber's Point in the long rolling surf.

Hawaii may be a tourist destination today; but it was not paradise to the marines in their training. "At night the mosquitoes were unbelievable." Ray later recalled.

> They were big enough to fly off with a small man. On the beaches, no mosquitoes . . . but the flies were incredible. And everything we ate had sand in it. It's surprising what you get used to.
>
> Companies A and B trained on this beach for approximately four weeks, the last of July and the first half of August. At first, the two companies trained on individual assignments of their part of the raid plan. In addition, daily training on the rubber boat landings were going on. The difficult part of the boat landings was the challenge of getting the rubber boats out to the sea, about one half mile from shore, fighting those huge ocean swells as they neared the beach—but with eight men paddling and the help of the motor, we were generally successful. The fun part was on our return to shore.

Like modern day surfers, Ray said, "we would try to get the rubber boat located on the crest of the wave and ride that wave all the way into shore without paddling or using the motor. It was exciting—something like organized grab-ass."

When Carlson's Raiders got liberty, Honolulu was the place to go. Many marines chose to go to the local bars, but others like Ray frequented the nonalcoholic businesses. Ray was too much in love with Lil to be tempted.

The Makin Island Raid

Carlson's objective for their target of Makin Atoll in the Gilbert Islands was to decimate enemy installations, secure vital information, and distract the Japanese from the Solomon Islands and Guadalcanal, which the United States planned to invade. These two companies of raiders, 221 men, departed Pearl Harbor on August 8, 1942, on two large submarines, the *Nautilus* and the *Argonaut*. Instead of their standard arsenal of mines and torpedoes, the two ships were stripped of most of their weapons store to carry the additional men and their equipment, in addition to their normal crew of 100 navy personnel. Living quarters were unbelievably cramped. As Ray noted in his diary, "Sardines have it easier, at least they have oil to move around in."

Living conditions were horrendous. Quarters were so crowded that about all the raiders could do was to lay in their bunks, play chess or cards, or just talk. There was almost no ventilation, so the heat and the smell were stifling. Ray felt lucky in that he stood watching on the conning tower of the sub at midnight every night for the nine days it took. "It got me out of the Hell hole that was below," he said.

For the most part, the subs ran on surface for the nine days and nights it took them from Pearl Harbor to the Gilbert Islands.

In the darkened predawn hours of August 16, the *Nautilus* and *Argonaut* reached a place called Makin Island in the Gilbert Island chain. The two companies of raiders disembarked from the submarines onto their rubber boats. Their green fatigues were dyed black. These landings were nothing like what they had practiced in Hawaii. It was raining, and Ray recalled that instead of the long rolling surf of Hawaii,

> The sea conditions were horrendous, strong currents and choppy waters—all of our training at Barbers' Point, for the most part, went out the window. The currents around Makin Island were like a swift river. Even the natives rarely sailed their boats on that side of the island. The current was so strong that the submarines could not stop, as the boat was pushed back.
>
> There were a hundred Marines standing on the deck, getting water washed over us by heavy seas. The deck got really slick, and we kept slipping. Then we had to inflate the rubber boats. That was a chore in those conditions. Then we had to put them over the side. We quite a time, trying to disembark. Sometimes the waves would make the rubber boats higher than the sub and then it would come down. Trying to put our equipment and rifles was quite a task. Then all of the boat motors would not work. We had to paddle in against the current. We were exhausted by the time we made shore, and luckily we made it there just before dawn.
>
> Getting the rubber boats ashore was also a real problem. If you didn't get the prow exactly straight facing the island, the waves would catch the boat sideways and turn it over. Soaking wet, cold and tired, we pulled the rubber boats up on the shoreline and covered them with brush. It was so dark you couldn't see the front of your hand. All that could be made out was the outline of the palm trees. The communication center we were supposed to hit was about thirty yards inland.

However, despite this set back, we had the training and ability to handle the rubber boats, make shore and work together as a unit. We were calm, efficient and went into combat as though nothing had occurred.

Company A's responsibility was to knock out Japanese communications, so they couldn't call out for help. Ray recalled,

> There was a rumor that one of our Marines hooked up with a Japanese girl in Hawaii before we left. He told her all about what the Raiders were going to do. It was later discovered that she was a Japanese spy. Once we were ashore though, things began to go badly.

Because of the deteriorating conditions, Carlson changed his plan, so they would all go ashore together rather than landing separately. One platoon commander didn't get the word. Lieutenant Oscar Petross and his squad landed alone in what became the enemy rear. To make things worse, one of the raiders accidentally discharged his weapon, ruining all hope of a surprise attack.

First Lieutenant Merwyn Plumbley led Ray's company. According to Ray,

> We ran and hit the ground hard, and crawled into a hole. Where we were fighting was the narrowest part of the Island. It wasn't even a mile wide . . . Maybe three hundred yards at that point. .you couldn't tell where the bullets were coming from, so I made it a point to make myself as small as possible.

In the actions that followed, the raiders made little advancement battling the enemy's fire power and snipers. Suddenly, the Japanese launched two **Banzai attacks**, accompanied by screams and bugles. Companies A and B easily shot down the two charging groups of Japanese.

This action changed every man in the Raiders. It is combat that forms a bond like no other. That bond is molded by training and friendship, and is forged by the fires of hell that is war. It is a bond so strong that not even death can break it. They thought of, but didn't talk about, the possibility of dying. On the front page of his diary Ray wrote, "In case of death, send this diary Mrs. C Bauml." As Ray later joked, "I was never scared. I was, though, concerned a lot."

Ray's fire team was made up of Ray, Ruben Hedger, and Bud Nodland.

His company suffered immediate casualties, as did Company B. Company B's Sergeant Clyde Thomason was killed in the initial action when he courageously made his way through enemy fire to redirect his platoon's fire. Sergeant Clyde Thomason was later posthumously awarded the Medal of Honor.

Three of the 10 men in Ray's squad were killed in that action. One was Corporal Daniel Gaston. Gaston had grown up an orphan; he is a tough guy from Brooklyn, New York. Ray used to help him write love letters to his many girlfriends. Corporal Harris Johnson, a schoolteacher from Iowa, was shot through the head. The third man, Bud Nodland, was the youngest and smallest in Company A; and he also carried the largest rifle, the **Browning automatic rifle**. It weighed 19 and a half pounds empty.

Bud always had to prove himself because of his size, but prove himself he did over and over. He was killed a month before his 19th birthday.

Following the first day of action, Ray was sent on a reconnaissance mission, looking for other raiders and stragglers. It was during this time he had his first real encounter with the native Butaritari people. They helped him with information about the whereabouts of the remaining Japanese.

These native people more than willingly helped Ray and the other Raiders, for the Japanese had destroyed their paradise home. The Butaritari volunteered their services. They carried the Marines' ammunition, and gave them pertinent information.

Some natives ignored enemy fire and supplied the marines with coconuts and coconut milk while informing them of Japanese movements. Most of the communications were done through an interpreter and impromptu sign language. Unbeknownst to Ray and the others at the time, they had nearly extinguished the entire Japanese garrison. The Raiders had killed 198 Japanese Marines. They had also destroyed three radio centers and over a thousand gallons of gasoline. They had decimated trucks and anything else that could have been of use to the Japanese.

The fighting wasn't over, though. Around 1130 hours, two Japanese planes were scouting the area. Carlson ordered his men to take cover, and not to fire on the planes as to give away their position. The planes bombed the area, but there were no casualties. Within two hours, 12 Japanese planes, including several large seaplanes carrying reinforcements arrived.

The raiders' machine guns and antitank rifles opened up on them, destroying one of the large seaplanes. For about an hour, the remaining Japanese planes bombed the island. But their ordinance (fire from bombs and guns) landed in areas not held by the Raiders.

Another air attack came later that afternoon when enemy reinforcements, able to elude attack, made it ashore. Fortunately, the *Argonaut* and the *Nautilus* sank the two enemy ships killing another 150 Japanese.

Toward the end of the fighting, the natives told Carlson there were only eight Japanese left alive on the island, all of them snipers. The raiders killed six, but never found the other two.

Carlson then began his plans for evacuation back to the two awaiting subs. The retreat was incredibly haphazard. There was no organization entering the subs. It was upon reaching Pearl Harbor before an accurate account of any casualties was made.

Communications were also poor. One of the real tragedies of the Makin Island attack was that nine raiders were left behind on the island in the chaos of the raid. But with the help of the Butaritari people, these men evaded capture for almost three weeks. They surrendered to Japanese reinforcements on August 30, 1942, and were removed from Makin Island. They were taken to the island Kwajalein. In October of the same year, these raiders were beheaded, out of revenge for that raid and the invasion of Guadalcanal that followed. Their bodies have never been found.

Carlson took his wounded with him, but he could not take those who had been killed. Before his withdrawal, Carlson, through an interpreter, asked the islanders if they would please bury the marine dead so that the Japanese could not find them. He paid the chief 50 dollars, although Ray said in retrospect the gesture really didn't make much sense. Where was the chief going to spend it? The chief wanted to help. No gifts and no payment were necessary.

Ray later noted in his diary, "The other Jap supplies were handed out to the natives, which tickled the hell out of them." It was during the trip back to Hawaii, that Ray found out that Gaston, Johnson, and Nodland had been killed.

Incredible stories about the action on Makin soon began to emerge. For example, one of the marine officers lost his pants during the fight and showed up on the beach wearing a native sarong.

Trying to leave the island in the rubber boats proved almost impossible for Ray and the others. The wounded aboard his boat slowed their progress as the group rowed head-on against a strong current. They were losing their battle against the forces of nature. Then Ray and the others witnessed something remarkable. The *Argonaut*'s captain turned the submarine around and began making his way toward the men in the rubber boats.

One of the men on Ray's raft had been wounded in the head. The seas were so rough that the water washed the man overboard. The medic with him, "Doc Stickler," dived into the water to rescue the man. Before Ray and the others reached the sub, the man was washed overboard two more times. Each time Doc Stickler dived in and brought the man back on the way to the sub. Ray remembered trying to hold on to the line from the sub, feeling his strength ebb away from him, when all of a sudden he heard a voice yell, "Hey **Jairene**, let go of the line and get your ass aboard!" When Ray turned and looked, he saw he was the last man on the rubber boat. All of the wounded and others had been evacuated.

Having wounded aboard, and nine more days to go on an incredibly cramped submarine made the return trip worse. The reality of war had just happened in living color. On August 23, 1942, Ray wrote in his diary,

I sometimes believe that the fellas that were killed on Makin have the best of the deal. In this outfit if we make many more raids, death is inevitable, plus the fact we have to travel in these God-forsaken sub-marines for many long, tedious and unending hours.

Word had spread throughout the United States that the raid on Makin was a major success. It was the first offensive land victory for the United States, just eight months after the attack on Pearl Harbor. This victory gave America huge boost to its morale. What the raiders did not foresee was how the public and even the rest of the Marine Corps and Navy would respond to their actions.

On August 26, 1942, Ray noted in his diary,

Met our escort and got into the harbor . . . we received quite a recep-tion. Two battleships lined up, plus each ship's band, plus sailors off several destroyers and subs; plus a platoon of Marine guards, plus Marine officers, photographers, bands etc. All the above-mentioned men were lined up on the docks, on shore cheered on while the vari-ous bands played the Marine Corps Hymn and several other stirring melodies. Everyone seemed to have their pictures taken and in short, it was a grand reception for the boys who returned from the Makin Raid.

The participants of the Makin Raid were treated to a three-day stay at the Royal Hawaiian Hotel, where Ray remembered,

At that point in time, this was considered the most exclusive and lux-urious hotel in the islands. The hotel was for those with lots of money. During the war the place was taken over by the government and was used, for the most part, for the service personnel that participated in submarine and aviations service. The fact that we had 18 days of submarine time to Makin and back, entitled us to this treat. Excellent food, comfort, use of the facilities—beaches, play rooms and what not, was like a breath of spring after those miserable, stinking days on a crowded sub. My time during the hotel stay was spent mostly drinking malted drinks and listening to Woody Herman's recording of the song "Wood Chopper's Ball" on the jukebox. Only one problem, there was always a cloud over one's head, thinking about those Raid-ers left on Makin. It took quite a while to get over it.

* * *

Back in Oak Park, Lillian Vosicky wrote to Ray constantly, and dreamed of his return. The song she listened to at every chance was Frank Sinatra's record-ing of "This Love of Mine."

But Ray didn't get home for almost two years.

After a brief respite in Hawaii and more training, Ray and Carlson's Raiders were sent to Guadalcanal, where they took part in the "Long Patrol," a 30 days behind the enemy lines patrol in which he saw almost constant combat. During that time, neither Ray's mother nor Lil heard from him at all. There was simply no time or place to sit and write anything.

After Guadalcanal, Ray and the Raiders were sent to Bougainville, again fighting behind enemy lines.

Ray and his company finally were ordered back to the United States in early 1944. On Valentine's Day, he sent Lil a telegraph that read, "Arrived States OK Maybe Wedding Bells will be ringing shortly."

Sure enough, Ray and Lil were married March 11, 1944, and he was transferred to Camp LeJeune, North Carolina, until the war's end. Initially, the couple moved back to Illinois where Ray went back to work for the Chicago, Burlington and Quincy Railroad. They had kept Ray's job for him, and he remained with the company until 1981, when he retired. That same year, Ray and Lil moved to Colorado, where they still reside as of this writing.

Glossary

Banzai attack: Sometimes a thousand Japanese soldiers charged the Marine positions shooting their guns and attacking with their fixed bayonets and Samurai swords. They always accompanied these attacks with blood-curdling screams and bugle calls.

Browning automatic rifle: One of the heaviest handheld machine guns.

Gunny: Nickname for Gunnery sergeant.

Jairene: A Marine derogatory slang nickname.

Tin can: Nickname for a U.S. Navy destroyer, smallest of the fighting ships (the difference between a ship and a boat is the length of the craft. Anything over 125 feet is classified as a ship. Anything under that length is classified as a boat).

Story Notes

This story is based on the recollections of Raymond and Lillian Bauml, delivered to me through a series of interviews between 2000 and 2010, some of which were filmed or taped, and Ray's diary, in which he kept his Makin Island experiences.

I have known Ray and Lillian for close to eight years (at this writing) and cherish the time I spend with them. Ray has allowed me to film his extensive interviews. There have been numerous military publications about Carlson's Raiders, but I have been fortunate enough to have not only exclusive taped interviews with Ray but also permission to use his never-before published photographs.

Ray's memory about times, places, and events has proven to be incredibly accurate. I have double checked many of the dates through the Marine Corps Raiders Museum in Quantico, Virginia, and have found no variances.

Chapter 15

No Greater Love:
Bryant Womack

The Korean War has been called the "Forgotten War" mostly by people who never served in the military or don't know the history of this country. In fact, the fighting was the most vicious of the 20th century. In three years of combat, over 53,000 Americans lost their lives and another 8,051 are still listed as Missing in Action. This story is about a North Carolina country boy who gave the ultimate gift to his fellow soldiers in one of the coldest winters ever recorded in Korea.

There is a place called Mill Spring. It isn't exactly a town. Mill Spring is located in Polk County, North Carolina, just over the Rutherford County line where the mountains, bottomless pools, waterfalls, and rivers all surround the area. Not many paved roads existed there in the first three decades of the 20th century, nor do they today. In the mid-20th century, few people in the area owned automobiles, let alone had ever seen one that wasn't a Model T or a Model A Ford. Far fewer had seen an airplane. Plows were still pulled by mules and horses, and most food was either hunted or grown.

Bryant Homer Womack was born on May 12, 1931, in this isolated area of Western North Carolina. The Great Depression had just begun and it made life even harder for the already poor Womack family.

Yes, times were hard, but times were always difficult for the people of this area. Moonshine was readily available. Folks in Mill Spring drank it—and they sold it. Just because it was against the law to purchase an alcoholic beverage in those days didn't mean that folks wouldn't purchase an illegal drink. It was one of the ways hill folk and mountain folk made the cash they needed to feed their families. In many parts of Western North Carolina, moonshiners like "Popcorn Sutton" still ply their trade, as did his father before him.

The closest city was Asheville, and it was a hard day's travel to get there. There were smaller towns where supplies could be purchased. Rutherfordton was the county seat. For 200 years, Rutherford County had been an historic hub in American history. Revolutionary War veterans settled the area back in 1791. Some 30 years prior to that, the Womacks settled in the area; and they have been there ever since. There were Womacks who fought in the Revolutionary War and later in the Civil War and every other war that followed.

Bryant grew up listening to the stories that filled the area. He thrilled to the stories about the Revolutionary War, and of the Womacks who fought in the Civil War.

North Carolina, one of the original 13 colonies and the surrounding counties in which Bryant lived, became an area of "firsts" in the United States; and Bryant heard about those firsts. The first gold strike happened by accident in Mecklenburg County about 50 miles away by a 12-year-old boy in 1799. The boy was fishing and saw a shinny object in the water. He picked it up out of the water and took it home. The nugget of gold he found was "the size of a small smoothing stone." The boy, Conrad Reed, gave the nugget to his father who didn't know what it was and kept the piece for several years as a door stop. Three years later John Reed, Conrad's father took the nugget into a local market and was informed of just what it was. The nugget was made into a large bar of gold that measured around 8 inches long. Not fully understanding what he had, John Reed sold it for $3.50.

The area where Conrad Reed found the "shiny stone" yielded a huge vein of gold. One nugget reportedly weighed 28 pounds.

With the gold strike came a need for assay offices and a branch of the U.S. mints. Christopher Bechtler, a German immigrant opened a mint located in Rutherford County and minted the first gold coin in U.S. history, a full 18 years before the Philadelphia mint was established.

Bryant also heard stories and legends of the mountains particularly the Cherokee stories about the "little people" who lived in the Bald Mountains. Most of the Cherokee people were forced out of North Carolina by Andrew Jackson and relocated in Oklahoma. Those that held out had established a reservation about 60 miles north of Bryant's home.

Other legendary characters appeared in stories throughout the areas of Polk and Rutherford counties. One local tale proclaims that Abraham Lincoln was the illegitimate son of a North Carolina man named Abraham Enloe, who held Nancy Hanks as an indentured servant. Other such tales claim that the remainder of the infamous outlaws the Dalton gang settled in Rutherford County. Court records clearly reveal some accuracy in both tales. Bryant knew many of the descendants of the Enloes and Daltons.

And as in most parts of the world, Polk, Rutherford, and the surrounding counties, ghost stories were told.

One of the most popular ghost stories took place in Rutherfordton. Seems the shadow of an innocent man who was hanged came back and haunted the jail professing his innocence. That shadow could be seen, it was reported, until the jail was torn down in 1962.

The most famous ghost story of all, though, was about the "Brown Mountain Lights." Every clear night, a light could be seen traveling throughout the mountain. The most popular version of the story featured star crossed lovers trying to find each other in the night. These lights have been purportedly seen for hundreds of years. The Cherokee reported seeing them long before whites settled in the area. Those who have seen them say that the lights seem twice as bright as a star and move erratically up and down Brown Mountain, often with a red or blue tint to them.

This story was so famous that musicians created a banjo piece about it. Bryant had heard the story and loved it; he loved the music even more.

By the time Bryant was 16 years old, he stood over 6 feet tall. Lanky and strong, Bryant was devoted to his mother Julie. He had three brothers and a sister. Bryant and his youngest brother George were constant companions. They loved to hunt and fish; and they learned how to trap and tan hides. They sold those pelts for whatever precious money they made to supplement what little other money the Womacks had. As soon as they returned home they handed the money over to their father.

As fond as he was of his mother and brothers, Bryant was never close to his father George Womack. As soon as he was old enough to walk, his father gave him chores to do, and then beatings, if his completed task didn't meet his father's expectations. Sometimes his father would just beat Bryant for no reason, and the only one to stop him was his mother.

Like most boys, Bryant and his brother loved to explore their surroundings; and of course, found ways of getting into trouble, and played practical jokes whenever they could. Almost no other children lived in the area. The boys' mischief did not go unnoticed—or unpunished. Bryant's beatings continued as he grew older, and his father forced him to leave school at the age of 16, while he was at the height of his school social life.

Bryant worked as a farm laborer, picking peaches and apples when they were in season. Being at home meant suffering under incredibly hard working conditions. What made life bearable for Bryant was music. He taught himself to pick a banjo and a guitar. A gifted musician, he played wherever and whenever he could. His only other respite from his father's tyranny was wandering the hills, rivers, and streams by himself.

As mentioned, Bryant adored his mother. Julie Womack had done her best to teach Bryant and his siblings to be thoughtful and courteous to everyone. She took them to church where they were taught the teachings and stories of the "good book."

Regardless of weather, Bryant walked two miles every day from the house down a country lane just to get to the road to hitch a ride or catch a bus so he could get to town.

As time passed and as Bryant got older, the beatings his father gave him became more frequent and vicious, but Bryant never raised his hand against him. The Bible taught him, "Thou shalt honor thy mother and thy father." Bryant was never a violent person.

Those who knew Bryant described him as very outgoing—someone who would go out of his way to help those he cared about. As a young man, he desperately needed to leave home though, if only to escape his father's cruelty, but there seemed no way out.

Finally, Bryant found a way out—the U.S. Army. By then Bryant had become a pacifist.

When he was younger Bryant had thought about the military, but at the time he was too young to enlist. WWII ended in 1945 when he was 14 years old. His father's abuse seemed to zenith when Bryant reached his 18th birthday. About that time America found herself in another war in another Asian land called Korea.

Harry Truman was still president of the United States; and just after the WWII the big fear was communism. The United States aligned herself with communist Russia during the war and now Russia appeared to want to control of not only eastern Europe, but extend her reach into China and North Korea. It was the beginning of the "Cold War."

That Cold War turned to hot and bloody on June 25, 1950, when communist North Korea invaded South Korea. President Truman along with the United Nations sent troops.

One night Bryant took off and made his way down into Rutherfordton and the army recruitment office. He told the recruiter he had talked to a friend about being in the Army, but confessed he did not want to harm anyone. The friend had told Bryant that he could join as a medic. They only helped soldiers.

So Bryant Womack joined the Army and was sent off to basic training. He received orders to go to Korea, and came home for a short furlough after basic training. He sought out friends and family. When he came home, the family greeted him fondly, except for his father. He did not speak to Bryant; he just glared at him.

Early the next morning Bryant left the house, but he stayed in the area. He camped out under a bridge at night so his father wouldn't know he was still around. It was the last time his family would ever see him.

Private first class Bryant Homer Womack entered the Medical Company of the 14th Regiment, 25th Infantry Division. Along with his division, he shipped off to Korea in the winter of 1952.

That year the Korean winter was brutal; unbelievably cold temperatures enveloped the U.S. troops. Supplies were insufficient for the extreme weather conditions. The marines nicknamed the Chosin Reservoir, where they were fighting, "the frozen Chosin."

On the night of March 12, 1952, near Soksori in an area the GIs called the "Punch Bowl" close to Heartbreak Ridge, Bryant was loaned out to another company. That's how a night patrol became legend in the life of the tall, lanky, country boy from North Carolina.

Bryant's sergeant, Sam Kupperson later recalled that Bryant Womack volunteered to go out with the patrol as the company medic. Kupperson remembered,

> That night the temperatures were brutal. You just couldn't stay warm . . . It was probably twenty below zero and we were up against superior forces.
>
> I had sent Bryant out when two of our guys stepped on a concussion mine which is meant to blow and seriously injure when all hell broke loose, Bryant immediately began tending to the wounded.
>
> The patrol then came under heavy machine gun fire and mortar attacks. When the explosions occurred and the firefight commenced, Bryant took off to help the wounded. This necessitated Bryant exposing himself to a devastating hail of enemy fire. As Bryant ran to the aid of the first wounded man, he himself was seriously wounded. I could see when Bryant was first hit, by the motion of his body. I learned later that he refused any medical aid for himself. He just moved on to the next man. Bryant continued moving and aiding the other wounded.

In the night flashes, Kupperson and others saw Bryant being shot over and over again. Then a mortar landed and exploded right next to Bryant while he aided the wounded. The explosion blew his right arm off just below the elbow. Even that didn't stop Bryant though, he continued on. He directed others in how to help him aid the wounded and gave them a crash course in how to stop the bleeding and how to dress their wounds. Even though his own injuries were more severe than those of the others, Bryant refused aid for himself. He insisted that he be the last to be evacuated.

After a while as Bryant walked unaided to the rear of that battlefield, he collapsed. Sam Kupperson grabbed Bryant and held him. Weakened by the loss of blood, Bryant told Sam, that the men who stepped on the concussion mine would be okay. And then weakly added, "I'll be okay too." He died in Sam Kupperson's arms.

When the fighting ended that night, Sam Kupperson was rotated out of that company. It wasn't until some months later that he found out that Private First Class Bryant Homer Womack was posthumously awarded the Medal of Honor. The citation in part reads, "The extraordinary heroism, outstanding courage, and unswerving devotion to his duties displayed by Pfc. Womack reflect the utmost distinction upon himself and uphold the esteemed traditions of the U.S. Army."

On January 7, 1953, Secretary of the Army Frank C. Pace presented the medal to Bryant's mother and father in Washington, D.C.

Bryant's body was returned home and he was buried in the Mill Spring Lebanon Church Cemetery.

Bryant's portrait was painted, and with great ceremony hanged in the Rutherford County Court House.

In 1969, a new army medical center in Fort Bragg, North Carolina, was named in honor of Bryant Homer Womack. Today it serves over 160,000 active duty service personnel and retired military.

Bryant Womack had been a giver in life. The men he served with were his friends. Before he was killed, maybe somewhere in the back of his mind he remembered something he heard in church or read in the Christian Bible, "Greater love hath no man than this; that a man lay down his life for his friends" (John 15:13).

Story Notes

I was first told the story of Bryant Womack by his relatives in North Carolina many years ago. Something came up in conversation when Bryant's nephew George Womack made the comment about, "Uncle Bryant won the Medal of Honor." My first reaction was, "What? What do you mean?" because I had learned a long time ago, that one doesn't "win" the Medal of Honor. One is awarded the Medal of Honor.

George then told me the story and shared much of his research into Bryant's life with me. He introduced me to Sam Kupperson, Bryant's sergeant, who now lives in Illinois.

The historic information in this story comes from my research in this area, starting back in the late 1970s to the present. I spent many an hour with the wonderful folks at the Rutherford County Historic Society. I lived in Rutherford County for eight years and still perform in the colleges there every couple of years. Other information came directly from the U.S. Army's military files. Today, much of that information can be found on the Internet.

Chapter 16

A Nurse's Story: Jonita Ruth Bonham

Women today are making their mark fighting war in Iraq and Afghanistan and demanding equality on the battle field; but, almost 400,000 women served in and with the armed forces during WWII. This story is about one of those women who went beyond her call of duty to save her fellow servicemen.

On the 11th hour of the 11th day of the 11th month in the year 1918, an armistice was signed to end what was, up till then, the world's worst war. And with the end of that war, the lives of millions of young Americans had dramatically changed.

The Victorian age had been pushed off the world's stage at bayonet point, as the jazz era was trumpeted in. The Roaring Twenties had arrived into life's theater, on April 3, 1922, Jonita Ruth Bonham was born in Oklahoma City, Oklahoma.

Jonita graduated from high school amidst the turmoil of the Great Depression and she always wanted to leave Oklahoma, the dust storms and subsequently enrolled in a nursing school. After graduating from nursing school, Jonita joined what was then called the Army Air Corps and was commissioned a 2nd Lieutenant in the medical corps during WWII. Jonita served in the Philippines and Japan just after the war. She returned to the United States and resigned from the military until the start of the Korean War. Without hesitation, she rejoined what was now called the U.S. Air Force as a 1st Lieutenant in September 1948. Soon after, she volunteered as a flight nurse in the medical air evacuation program. Their aircraft was a C-54 cargo plane that had been converted into a miniature hospital emergency room. They would leave Japan with replacement combat troops, fly them to Kimpo, Korea, and then bring back and care for the wounded headed for the military hospitals in Japan. The aircraft were constantly under enemy fire by North Korean troops, both on take offs and landings.

One night, during the time Jonita was serving, her parents attended a movie where a newsreel about the Korean War was shown. During the newsreel, their daughter, Lieutenant Jonita Ruth Bonham, an air evacuation nurse, appeared on screen stepping off her plane—a C-54—in Korea. A few days later, they received a telegram. The telegram sent the proud and happy Bonhams into total shock, as they read that Jonita was ". . . seriously ill in a Japanese hospital since September 26, when she was injured in an aircraft accident."

That's all the telegram said. It made no mention that 26 people, including the pilot and the other flight nurse, Vera Brown, were killed in the "accident." Vera had been sitting next to Jonita. The telegram also didn't tell them about the kind of hours the flight teams were putting in and the conditions around them. In the two weeks previous to the crash, Jonita and her crew had been aloft for 245 hours and had evacuated over 600 wounded from Korea to hospitals in Japan. There had been no days off or sleep for her crew, except for the token three hour naps in between flights. The telegram didn't mention the amount of enemy fire their plane took every time it landed.

In fact, the first taste of Jonita's reality reached the Bonhams when they received a message from Major Clifford Boveé:

> Your daughter is making a splendid recovery from the injuries she sustained in the airplane crash last Tuesday morning. She suffered a broken left forearm, a fracture of the right shoulder blade and some painful lacerations of the scalp, with, of course, a general shaking up and numerous bruises and scratches. However, there is nothing critical nor of a permanent nature about her condition. . . .

His letter continued giving information about what hospital she was in and when she would be transferred to Tokyo. On the second page he described how the crash occurred; and then mentioned what Jonita had done immediately after the plane crash.

> You may be very proud of your splendid daughter. She won the respect and admiration of everyone for her courage, bravery, resourcefulness and clear thinking during the disastrous tragedy. Following the crash, and despite her own suffering, she reacted so quickly to the emergency that she succeeded in getting life rafts launched and directed their loading during the few moments before the plane sank. Had it not been for her courage and presence of mind, it was the unanimous opinion of all that there would not have been half the survivors there were from there the crash. I trust there is nothing contained in this

letter which may give you any cause for alarm, for rest assured that you need have none . . . She will be hospitalized for probably two or three weeks to allow the fractures to knit.

Within 10 days the Bonhams received another letter dated Saturday, September 7, 1950, this time from Jonita, who never mentioned what she had done.

> Dear Mother and Daddy, I haven't heard from you all since the plane crash, but I know I shall just most any time—and since I feel pretty good today I'm going to try and write you all about it. I hope you can read this scribbling, but I'm flat in bed and my right arm is broken at the shoulder, so I can't move it except for the fingers. My left wrist is broken too—so when they put my right shoulder in a splint I'm not going to able to do anything. One thing I didn't tell you—I got a skull fracture out of the accident, but I've already had the surgery done, and it's perfectly all right. I also got a big cut on my cheek, which is going to call for a little plastic work. It's really not bad at all, tho' as it is—I shall be coming back to the states tho' sooner. And I'm absolutely through with flying—which you will be probably glad to hear. Our crash was on take off and we crashed into the water. We were taking troops into Kimpo. There were about 50 some on the plane & about 28 of us were saved. So—see, I really was very lucky . . . If they splint my arm soon I'll have the Red Cross write you soon. Love Always, Jonita (Bonham, 1950.)

Again, Jonita understated the extent of her injuries. Even though she said nothing about her actions in the early morning hours of September 26, 1950, word of her heroics began pouring out from crash survivors, not only to the press but also to Air Force officials.

Private First Class Percy Johnson, who was a hardened combat veteran who survived the crash, returning to the front lines of Korea, and wrote in his official report to the Air Force:

> Lieutenant Bonham took command. None of us guessed that she was badly hurt. She wasn't excited and she used her head. All the men took orders from her without question. She saved a lot of guys. (Boveé, 1994)

And the facts were more incredible than fiction. In the early morning hours of September 26, 1950, Lieutenant Jonita Bonham woke up from her three-hour nap. She heated up and drank two strong cups of black coffee—the kind that would take rust off a 40-year-old wreck. After her brief respite of coffee, Jonita headed for flight operations. When she stepped outside, she noticed the wind. It began howling through the compound. The wind felt and blew as though a storm was in the brewing, but there was no rain. When Jonita reported to flight operations in the darkness of predawn, she could hear the throbbing engines of a half dozen cargo planes as they idled on the runway. They were all lined up for takeoff.

Once inside the operations building, Jonita met with Lieutenant Vera Brown. She and a medical technician were the other two members of her team. Outside, Jonita and Vera could see hundreds of soldiers waiting to board the other cargo planes. Forty-seven soldiers were already aboard Jonita's C-54. Their normal routine was anything but normal. After the returning troops were unloaded, the wounded would be immediately loaded. Time was of the essence, for much of the time while flying into the landing zones, unloading troops, loading the wounded, and then taking off again; they were almost always under heavy enemy fire. On this day, once Jonita and Vera boarded their plane, the pilot, told Jonita and Vera to try to get some sleep. But neither was ready. They sat next to each other and talked as the big engines of the C-54 began to roar and moved down the runway. The plane slowly began to climb into the air as it left the runway and up over the shores of the Sea of Japan. After the plane was about a half a mile from shore, it suddenly stalled and dropped from the sky. The C-54 slammed into the Sea of Japan. The impact made an awful noise as the whole aircraft immediately began to submerge. The force of the crash also caused the huge cargo plane to break into three pieces. Jonita found herself completely underwater and fought with all of her strength for the surface. Once she made it and gasped her first breath of air, Jonita, in total darkness listened as water began to swallow up the cargo plane. Desperately, she fought to keep herself above the water and to escape the confines of what was left of the aircraft. What made things worse was that the wind had whipped the sea into a churning mass of danger. Kicking her legs with all of her might to keep afloat, Jonita was finally able to grab onto a floating barracks bag that floated past. Some of the men around her were swimming, while others "floated in the water terribly still." For the first half minute, everything around her was very quiet. Then a voice out of the dark brought Jonita back into the world of sound.

"There's a life raft here," a man shouted, "how do you inflate it?" Without hesitation, Jonita yelled back, "Yank it out of its case and it will inflate itself!" Then she took command of the situation. The pilot and copilot were dead; Vera Brown had vanished (Boveé, 1994).

The next moment, Jonita saw the silhouette of the raft bounce high on a wave. She let go of the barracks bag and began to swim toward the raft, as did about a half dozen men. One of the men close by saw Jonita and screamed to the others, "Here's one of the nurses!" She felt an arm pushing her toward the raft. Once she reached the raft, she grabbed the rope that trailed from the vessel and then chose to stay in the water. Jonita shook the water from her face and eyes and began looking for others who were still in the water. She could see the surface of the waters spotted with the heads of swimming men.

Jonita then reached out to the closest man and grabbed him and guided his fingers toward the life rope. Then she found another and then another until she had 17 men with her. All were able to get onto the raft, except Jonita. In the darkness, she could make out another life raft about 20 yards away and saw men getting into it. Once Jonita was sure that everyone who had survived was on one of the life rafts, she allowed some of the men to reach down into the cold churning waters and drag her up over.

When she lay back in the crowded raft, the pain hit her like a large hammer. Her head and chest throbbed as a wave of nausea hit. Jonita's left arm hurt something fierce; and as she held it up, she could see that her wrist was bent to one side. She knew it was broken, but she didn't have time to worry about it. She was responsible for the lives of the survivors in the two rafts and Jonita didn't know how long. One man in the raft panicked and shouted he was going to swim for it, but Jonita commanded him to stay on the raft, "This water is full of sharks. Besides you'd be blown out to sea in this weather. Take it easy, soldier" (Boveé, 1994).

Ironically, no one at base operations knew the C-54 had crashed. As the life rafts floated, Jonita and the others could see the other planes taking off from the airstrip, but none of the planes could see through the darkness of the sea. Many of the 17 men with her were seriously injured. In rough seas and with water pouring into the two rafts, it was impossible for Jonita to give first aid. What she could do though was comfort them and keep the other survivors busy by shouting orders to them. Forgetting her own injuries, Jonita talked panicked men out of jumping into the water, and kept encouraging them to stay calm until her throat was raw.

After they were in the water for a couple of hours, one of the men saw a light. Sure enough, there was a light and its reflection cut across the waves.

"Start yelling!" Jonita ordered. "Everybody yell!" She again commanded. "All together! Everybody on both rafts! Keep on yelling!" Jonita knew that there was a slim chance they would be heard above the sea's waves and the wind. The light vanished for a moment then reappeared. Those who could shout continued to as their voices rolled on through the darkness and over the watery abyss below them. Little by little the craft with the light came nearer. Jonita could make out its form as it approached. It was a Japanese fishing vessel. As the boat approached, some of the men in the raft began to scramble up, ready to leap to safety, but again Jonita's voice rang through the air with a command.

"Stay where you are! You'll capsize us. Here pass this line to them. Show them the other raft" (Boveé, 1994). Once Jonita saw that both rafts were secured to the fishing boats and felt the jerk of the lines, she was able to relax a little.

Everything went dim for her, but she was not unconscious. The last thing she remembered was reaching shore. The next thing she saw was the inside of the hospital. And that's all she would see for the next nine months.

Jonita's injuries were extensive, including a broken cheekbone. When it was discovered she needed more than just one surgery on her head, she was eventually transferred to Maxwell Air Force Base Hospital in Alabama. However, by this time, the news had already been broadcasting Jonita's life story all over the United States—how she was born and raised in Oklahoma City and went to nursing school there. How she enlisted in what was then called the Army Air Corps and commissioned as a 2nd Lieutenant in the Medical Corps during WWII. And, how she stayed in the Philippines and Japan just after the war ended. Also, that she left the military for a short time and when the war in Korea broke out, and that she had no hesitation in volunteering her services again. She was now a 1st Lieutenant and her face was being seen around the nation.

One day, after she had undergone her third head surgery, Jonita was notified that Lieutenant General George Stratemeyer was coming for a visit. This really bothered her because she didn't have any hair. It had all been shaved off because of her surgery. A friend found a nice scarf that could be tied around her head. Jonita couldn't for the life of her think of why a general would want to see her. If she hadn't been so incapacitated with her shoulder and arm cast, Jonita would have fallen out of the bed she was in when she found out the reason for his visit.

General Stratemeyer presented Jonita with the Distinguished Flying Cross (DFC)—the highest decoration for valor that the Air Force bestows. Had Jonita been in Korea when the crash occurred, she probably would have been given the congressional Medal of Honor—but she would have had to have been in a combat zone to be eligible that decoration. As it was, Jonita, in her hospital bed had the DFC pinned on her pajamas by General Stratemeyer. This made Jonita Ruth Bonham the only woman in the history of the Korean War to be the recipient of the Air Force's highest award for valor.

Once the news got hold of this story and the accompanying photo (taken at the time of the ceremony in the hospital) America had a new but genuine hero. Newspapers and magazines had her face on their covers. *Everywoman's Magazine* and *Reader's Digest* both ran stories on Jonita. Then on April 9, 1952, *The Cavalcade of America* radio program aired Jonita's story. It starred the movie actress Nina Foch as Jonita (who was called Bonnie in those days). Millions of Americans heard her story and later a movie *Flight Nurse* was made about Jonita's experiences. In person though, Jonita didn't like to brag about anything she accomplished. She didn't allow the Hollywood hype to affect her demeanor.

Shortly after her being presented with the DFC, Jonita was promoted to captain. Major Clifford Boveé, the officer who was with Jonita shortly after her crash—and the same man who wrote the letter to her parents—married Jonita.

Jonita's injuries caused her considerable pain for some time; and the Air Force eventually gave her a full medical retirement from the service. For years after, while raising her family, she traveled the world with her husband Cliff, who remained in the military. They finally retired in Colorado Springs, Colorado.

On December 24, 1994, Jonita Ruth Bonham-Boveé quietly passed away from an insidious killer, cancer, in the home of her daughter Renee. Her story, like all heroes' stories, has faded in the minds of all except those whom she saved and those who loved her. She was a gentle and fun-loving woman who returned to flying. Jonita loved her family and enjoyed her special friends. Although she enjoyed the beauty of the ocean, she never again ventured into its waters.

Story Notes

I met Jonita's daughter, Renee, in the late 1980s, when I was working as an artist-in-residence for the Wyoming Arts Council. She was the performing arts program coordinator. Renee became aware of my interest in telling the stories of veterans, and when her mother died in 1994 she shared her story so I could retell it. Her story is unique but at the same time very typical of many people who serve in the military, Renee's mother said "They weren't heroes, they just did what they had to do."

Portions of this story are reprinted from Patrick Mendoza, Extraordinary People in Extraordinary Times: Heroes, Sheroes, and Villains. *Englewood, CO: Libraries Unlimited. Copyright © 1999 Patrick Mendoza.*

Chapter 17

The Day "Doc" Goss Became a Nurse: Jim Goss

Although much has been written about the Vietnam War, very little of it has focused on the common everyday enlisted men who are the true heroes of Vietnam, and of all other wars. The following story is about one such hero, Navy Corpsman James Goss.

In 1950, Jim Goss was a toddler amongst baby boomers in the small Pennsylvania town of Oxford in Chester County. He grew up in a time when Ford and Chevrolet ruled the automobile industry and when suburbia began her landscape sprawl across America. Yet, things remained somewhat unchanged in rural Pennsylvania, particularly in the rolling hills and farmlands in the surrounding Quaker countryside. Each town and hamlet had Friends Meeting Houses. And just across the county line, 20 miles away, was Lancaster county, home of the numerous Amish communities.

Jim's father, Joseph Goss was a WWII veteran and his background values were those of Middle America. He, like the others of his generation, had survived the Great Depression and then went to war. They came home to forever change the face of America. Joseph Goss's generation was responsible for the greatest economic growth this country has ever experienced.

In this same year, 1950, the United States established Military Assistance Advisory Groups, and sent them to their French allies in Southeast Asia to a place called French Indochina. North Korea invaded South Korea on June 25. Two days later, President Truman authorized the use of U.S. troops to assist. The Korean War was officially underway.

In 1963, troops were being sent to Vietnam, formerly known as French Indo-China. Ever since 1959, the United States had been sending more "military advisors" there to protect French interests and support the South

Vietnamese government from the North Vietnamese Communists; but few Americans were aware of the small country.

Since his inauguration as president of the United States, President John F. Kennedy had escalated U.S. troop buildup in Vietnam; although by 1963, he was considering the fact that maybe the United States shouldn't be there. The country and history will never know exactly what Kennedy would have done, because on November 22, 1963, Lee Harvey Oswald assassinated the president in Dallas, Texas.

Jim Goss was in room 210 at Oxford Area High School taking a business math class when the news of the tragedy was announced over the school's loud speakers.

Jim vividly remembers everything about that day, including a student sitting behind him who loudly professed his pleasure of the president's death. The math teacher, Mr. Meyers, quickly removed that student from the classroom, explaining that regardless of one's political views, there was nothing good about the murder of an American president. Political differences should be handled with the ballot, not a bullet.

Vice President Lyndon B. Johnson, one of the most powerful politicians of the 20th century, was sworn in as president; but his views on Vietnam later became the reason for his downfall.

With the exception of the American Civil War a hundred years before, the 1960s became the most turbulent times in American history. By now, 15-year-old Jim Goss had attended public schools and lived a life relatively free of troubles, beyond teenage acne and hormones.

In August 1964, a news event in the Gulf of Tonkin changed the face of American news reporting. Jim Goss and the rest of the world were told that North Vietnamese patrol boats attacked the American destroyers the *Maddox* and the *Turner Joy*.

Second Class Gunner's Mate, Michael Peters, was aboard the USS *Harry Hubbard* (DD-748) in the Gulf of Tonkin when the patrol boats were attacked. The crew affectionately nicknamed the ship "The Mother Hubbard."

Peters later remembered,

> We were 180 degrees out from the *Turner Joy* and the *Maddox*. We were part of a nine-ship carrier taskforce, along with the *Maddox* and *Turner Joy*. As soon as the attack on *Maddox* and *Turner Joy* took place, our ship went to number 3 alert . . . [meaning the crew is at almost full battle-stations.] "Battle stations" are what the Navy calls General Quarters.
>
> Everyone on the *Hubbard* was dressed in combat gear, but only one gun mount was completely manned. [Mike Peters captained the five-inch gun.] There were 18 men that manned the gun mount. (Peters, 1995)

Peters recalled that the *Hubbard* remained off the coast of Vietnam until September.

Because of this incident, President Lyndon Johnson authorized unrestricted bombing missions over North Vietnam. Within eight months, the marines landed just north of Da Nang.

Instead of heavy enemy fire on their beach landing, the 9th Marines witnessed sightseers, South Vietnamese officers, young Vietnamese girls, and four fellow soldiers with a large sign reading: "Welcome, Gallant Marines." The commander of all U.S. forces in Vietnam was General William Westmoreland. Back in the States, on all the radio stations, one song became an incredible hit in the year 1965, from a totally unexpected source. Army Green Beret Staff Sergeant Barry Sadler wrote and recorded the song, "The Ballad of the Green Beret." In just five weeks. *Billboard* magazine reported that the song sold over two million copies. Support for the Vietnam War in this country was at an all time high. Thousands of young men joined the Army to become Green Berets, although few qualified.

Something else changed that year in the war. News coverage was uncensored, and correspondents with cameramen began recording everything that was happening in Vietnam, and sending it back to the United States to be aired on television.

Vietnam War became the first televised war in history; the nightly coverage of the war had an incredible affect on the American public.

Jim Goss was part of that audience. Over the next few years, some Americans protested the war; and some were totally apathetic. And then there were the young men who either joined the military or were drafted into the Army.

The summer of 1967 was called "The Summer of Love." It also brought race riots and war protests; support for the war began to wane. Protest songs like, "I Feel Like I'm Fixin' to Die" and "Waist Deep in the Big Muddy" filled the pop charts of America's radio station. The country was in the midst of a culture war.

In August of that year, 19-year-old Jim Goss enlisted in the U.S. Navy. He felt he had to give something back to his country, as his patriotic duty. His father was a navy veteran, as was Jim's older brother Joe. The Navy was part of a family tradition.

Jim though, also felt a need to do more than just serve. Because of his local involvement in medical rescue in Oxford's Volunteer Fire Department, he wanted to help others the way they did.

Time and time again, he'd watched in awe as these men rescued people who were in horrifying situations. There were no emergency medical technicians in those days, just highly trained firefighters doing what they could in life and death situations. Now, Jim felt a calling into the field of medicine.

After attending boot camp at the Great Lakes Naval Station, Jim volunteered for Hospital Corpsman School.

As a Hospital Corpsman, Jim was trained to care for the sick and injured, administering immunizations and emergency medical procedures. The corpsmen also took care of medical records, filled and dispensed prescriptions, and took and processed X-rays. Normally the Corpsmen were sent out to the fleet or to naval hospitals or clinics; and sometimes they were sent to isolated naval facilities in lieu of a doctor or nurse.

Many times, though, they were transferred to the Marine Corps battalion, as the marines have no medical corps of their own.

Shortly after graduating from the Hospital Corpsman School at Great Lakes Naval Hospital, the Navy transferred Jim to Camp Lejeune in North Carolina to be trained in Marine Corps weaponry and survival skills. Then, in March 1969, Jim received his orders to report to Alpha Company, 1st Battalion 7th Marine Regiment of the 1st Marine Division.

Jim was now a navy sailor attached to the Fleet Marine Force. Normally this would be a nightmare, given the 200 years of rivalry between these two services, but Jim was a corpsman and corpsmen were special. Upon arriving in Vietnam, marine green was the given color to all. The young marines, as well as the older noncoms and officers were now "his boys" in the field; and he was "Doc." The villagers whom Doc Goss treated occasionally respectfully called him "*Bak si*" (doctor).

Jim's 19 weeks in Corpsman school could not have prepared him for the carnage that awaited him in Southeast Asia's jungles. Jim witnessed and treated wounds that emergency room physicians in this country, with 12 years of education, never dreamed of seeing. And he treated those men while he was being shot at.

Vietnam is a long way from Oxford, Pennsylvania. Upon arriving in country, the first thing Jim noticed was the smell. To him, it smelled like death. Anyone who ever served there would probably understand. It was, and is, a beautiful country; but the heat, the decay of rotting vegetation, and poor sanitation brewed a powerful stench.

The foliage is lush and green with palm and banana trees and vines with long thorns. The GIs called them "wait a minute vines." When going through them thorns often snagged clothing, the person being snagged was almost pulled completely back as if the vine were saying, "wait a minute!"

There are only two seasons in the country, the wet season and the dry season. No matter what the season, Jim and the others couldn't stay dry. In the dry season, Jim's clothes were soaked with sweat; and in the wet season, the rains seemed endless. The country's rivers were brown and most were filled with leeches.

The wildlife was amazing. In some parts of the country, soldiers saw Asian elephants and tigers. In every village and rice paddy, water buffaloes labored for the Vietnamese. And there were snakes, almost all of them poisonous, including bamboo vipers and cobras. The villagers lived much like their ancestors had, off the land. And for most of the 5,000 years of Vietnamese history, the people had been at war in one way or another.

In late 1969, North Vietnamese Regulars overran the firebase where Jim was stationed, just outside of Da Nang. During that firefight, Jim held compresses with one hand and his .45 semi-automatic pistol with his other hand. He covered the wounded with his own body while trying to keep them alive. In the middle of this chaos, he defended himself and his patients. With adrenaline running through his body, Jim did not know how bad that shrapnel from a rocket-propelled grenade (RPG) had wounded him until hours later when he went to get a shower. That's when the pain seared through his body and he saw his own blood turning the shower water red as it made its way into the drain.

For his valor under fire, Jim Goss received the Bronze Star Medal; and for his wounds he received the Purple Heart. From his "boys," he received their undying thanks and love.

Though the U.S. Military had been fully integrated in 1948, racial tensions of the 1960s made their way into Vietnam, but Jim didn't recall any in his company during his time in country.

In April 1970, after 13 months in Vietnam, Jim returned home. His fiancé, Kathy, remembered meeting him at the Philadelphia airport. "I didn't recognize him. He was coconut brown and he'd lost sixty pounds."

Jim and Kathy got married and settled back in Jim's hometown of Oxford, Pennsylvania. He found employment as a parts manager at an automobile dealership. He worked there for five years before deciding to attend nursing school. Two years later, Jim graduated with an associate degree. That was the day "Doc" Goss became a nurse. He ended up working in the emergency rooms of several hospitals, and also managed a paramedic unit for the local fire department.

Unbeknownst to Jim, life would bring him full circle. In 1997, he went to work for the U.S. Veteran's Hospital in Coatsville, Pennsylvania. He began working in the posttraumatic stress disorder (PTSD) unit that he headed until his retirement on April 30, 2010. He also continued on with his schooling, eventually earning a bachelors of science degree in nursing.

Perhaps unsurprisingly, Jim relates well with most of his patients, as many are Vietnam veterans. Nothing has really changed with Jim; he still takes care of "his boys." And though he is their charge nurse, they still call him "Doc." The name he earned in Vietnam.

Story Notes

I've known Jim Goss for over 20 years. This is not just his story, it is my tribute to all navy corpsmen, army medics, the nurses, and doctors who served in the combat theaters in which America was and is involved. God bless 'em all.

This story is based on my own experiences and recollections of my military service in Vietnam, as well as on those of Jim Goss and the many Vietnam veterans I have known. I've spent many hours talking with Jim about his experiences, and have also talked with his wife Kathy. I also interviewed Master Chief Gunner's Mate, Michael Peters, who not only was at the Gulf of Tonkin, but also served two other tours on the rivers of South Vietnam. Like Jim, I have known Michael Peters for many years.

Chapter 18

Pardo's Push: Bob Pardo

Some stories are best told by the source. This is a word-for-word transcrip-tion of Bob Pardo's presentation, as videotaped by the author in 2003, in Pigeon Forge, Tennessee, at the annual "Celebrate Freedom" event.

"In February of 1967, President Johnson said 'Okay boys, we're going to crank up the heat in North Vietnam. We're going to start hitting industrial targets.' Up until that time, we weren't hitting much of anything. We were making road cuts, trying to bomb bridges on small rivers, cut the Ho Chi Min trail, stop the supplies from going south . . . mostly just interdiction work. And he said now we were going to go for industrial targets. The first target on the list to be struck on March 1st was the Thai Nguyen Steel mill, 20 miles northwest of Hanoi.

All the forces in Thailand were technically not in the war. Due to the polit-ical situation, we weren't talked about. Where the people in the U.S. thought all the forces were coming from that were actually fighting in North Vietnam was anybody's guess. At any rate, we had a number of bases in Thailand support-ing F105 fire bombers. We were flying out of Ubon, Thailand in F4 [a type of fighter jet used during the Vietnam War], which played a multirole. Because of the versatility of the aircraft, we would carry iron bombs and missiles. And we would fly in among the F105s to cover them in the event that they were attacked by MiGs. And if they were, then we were to jettison our bombs and defend the F105s and let them continue onto the target and let them drop their bombs.

For the first nine days, we had trouble getting to the target because of bad weather in the target area. However, that didn't keep us from going. Every morning we would saddle up. All the airplanes were loaded up, and our instruc-tions were you will fly this route at this time and arrive at the target at such and such a time. And to make a long story short, we did that for nine days straight at exactly the same time of day, same route every day. The gunners on the ground, of which on March 1st there were 185 guns within five miles of target. By March 9th, they had moved in 25 percent of their anti-aircraft weapons. They now had 1,000 artillery bases within five miles of target and they had moved in six mobile surfaced air missile sites. The target was within 25 miles of two different MiG bases. And so this was a really bad place to be going day after day.

Not all of their guns were radar-trapping guns; some of them were just straight tubes, iron sites. But these guys were very good. They had been at it for a long time. They could shoot at sound if you were flying at night, and were successful at that. They probably downed as many airplanes at night shooting in the dark as they did in the daylight. And like Colonel Gantt said yesterday in his presentation, they were all nine level gunners. They were really good at what they did.

Finally on March 10th, the weather broke and it looked like we were going to put the bombs on the target finally. One of the flight members had a problem with his airplane and he had to abort on the ground.

We get airborne, and we're on the refueling tanker, and the ground spare that had filled in couldn't get the fueling door open, so he had to abort. So here comes our airborne spare, and he can get his door open, he gets some gas, and away we go off to the target. Now the airborne spare was being flown by a fellow named Earl Aman. We were both captains at the time. He was an Air Force Academy grad. Not a real close personal friend, he was just a squadron buddy just like the other guys in the flight.

There were four airplanes in the flight. We joined up with about eight flights of F105s and another flight of F4s. Now what we would do is position a flight of F4s right behind the lead flight of F105s and the second flight of F4s would fly tail end Charlie. And that's where I always ended up was tail end Charlie. That makes it fun because all the gunners get a lot of practice on these guys upfront before you get there, so they've got it pretty well thinned down before you arrive.

About 20 miles north of the target, we were at what we call the initial point where we start our final run-in for the bomb run. Ordinarily, we navigate in at about 420 knots and over the initial point; we push it up to about 480. So the faster you're going, the more it compounds the problems for the gunners. This day, after having flown through there so many times, the mission commander was even getting jumpy, and we were running at 630 knots and could barely keep up with the strike force. We could go into after-burner and the airplane wouldn't even accelerate. We were up against what we call compressibility. That's where you're pushing so much air in front of the airplane; it just won't go any faster no matter what you do to it.

At any rate, over the initial point, the number 4 man, Captain Aman, took hit from the anti-aircraft fire. But he didn't tell anybody. He and his back-seater talked it over. They didn't have any warning lights on; the airplane was flying fine, so they elected to continue with the mission. They took turns, they had already taken turns flying the airplane, while the other prayed—because apparently a number of us had had a premonition about this particular day. But they decided to continue on with the mission. They could have turned and gone out right there probably without any further damage and come on home. But we continued on into the target. And as we rolled in on the target, we cruise in somewhere between 10 and 12,000 feet. Varying the altitude, keeping the others working, compounding problem for the tracking radars, etc. But because of some clouds, we were forced down to about 8,000 feet. To start the bomb run we needed to be at about 14,000 feet and about 500 knots. And so we had to climb back up, and just as we start rolling in, Captain Aman took another hit. And this one was a pretty good one. But he's directly over the target, and again, rather than just rolling wings level and flying on out, he decided he would continue to attack the target.

As we pulled off the target, I took a hit in the belly of the airplane somewhere. All of our warning lights came on, except firelights. But our main objective at that point was to simply get the formation back together and get into what we called pod formation.

By that time we had jammers that operated against the surfaced air missiles and against some of the radar-tracking guns. We had to have our airplanes within about 1,000 feet of one another. So what we would do is spread out a four-ship formation with 1000-foot separation, and jamming would overlap each airplane and hopefully protect everybody. So what we were trying to do as soon as you come off target is get back in pod formation, flight integrity, and get the jammers going and keep the missiles off you if you can.

Also, one of the first things we did when coming off the target was to make a fuel check to see if anybody was hurting for gas. Coming off the target, we should have had 7,000 pounds of fuel remaining which was enough to make it all the way back to the first airfield we could get to. And when we made fuel check I was 2,000 pounds short and Captain Aman was 5,000 pounds short. In other words, he had 2,000 pounds of gas left, which meant right then and there that there was no way he was going to make it out of north Vietnam.

Now, the Hanoi area and our egress route [flying route in and out of the area] is all delta [where all the rivers come together into the South China Sea]. And if you go down there, one of two things is going to happen. If you're captured by civilians you're going to be killed or if you're captured by the militia or the military, you're going to jail. Neither of which are very satisfactory solutions to somebody flying along in a good airplane that is just a little short of gas.

So as we were egressing [flying to] the target, we couldn't keep up with the other two—the flight leader and the element leader—because Earl realized he had to stretch his gas as far as he could. So I lagged back with him and he started climbing for altitude, so when the airplane did flame out (when the engine looses it ability to fly and the leftover kerosene shoots a flame) he would get the best possible glide inside of it. And as we were climbing up to altitude, he starts jettisoning everything off the airplane to make it lighter so that it will glide further, climb better, so forth. I jettisoned all my bomb racks but kept my missiles because I thought okay if we get jumped by the MiGs on the way out, I've got enough gas to make about one turn and fire missiles and maybe run them off and give him a chance to get a little bit further out before they have to punch it.

Well, luckily the MiGs didn't chase us out that day. But when we got to altitude, or as we were approaching about 30,000 feet, I started asking myself what can we do here to get him out of this delta area and at least in the jungle over in Laos. The F4, as all fighters of that era, had a drag chute. And the drag chute compartment is located right in the very tail end of airplane. And for an airplane of that size, it takes a fairly good-sized parachute, so the drag chute compartment is about a foot in diameter. And I thought okay, if he jettisons the drag chute, perhaps I can ease in behind him and get the nose of my airplane— the radome—in the drag chute compartment and push him.

We had him jettison the drag chute, and as we started moving up behind him, of course the wash coming up off the upper surface of the wing and the tail was so great that turbulence behind him was such that we couldn't even touch him. We could get within 4–5 feet and the turbulence was so bad that we had to back away.

So we backed off and we dropped down and got underneath him and started looking at the belly of the airplane. And I thought maybe we can play Thunderbird here for a little bit. We'll just fly a little closer formation than they do. We'll get up underneath him and put the top of our fuselage up against the belly of his airplane and support him in that manner. And we're about 10 feet in under the airplane and as we started coming up next to him, we get about a foot from his fuselage and I could feel a vacuum pulling us together. And I said, if we allow it to slam into him, we could jam our canopies, because it was obvious by that point that we too were going to have to eject, because we were losing fuel and there was no way we were going to make it to the refueling tanker. So again we had to abandon that. And as we backed out from under him I'm looking at the bottom of his airplane and I noticed the tail hook.

This was primarily used by navy aircraft for landing aboard carriers. As they come aboard, the hook is extended from the bottom of the airplane and it grabs steel cable stretched across the deck and that allows them to stop in about 100 feet. Our airplanes were navy airplanes. The Air Force had bought the same airplane that the Navy had. Our runways were equipped with steel cables, so that if you came in with hydraulic failure, no brakes, you could use the hook, take the barrier, and the fire trucks knew exactly where you were going to be if you had any kind of emergency that you landed and used the hook.

Well, the hook extends down about 5–6 feet beneath the airplane. And I thought well perhaps that will be down below most of the wash coming off the underside of the airplane. By this time he's flamed up. He's run out of gas. The F4 when it glides, you glide at 250 knots and it's coming down at about 3,000 feet a minute. So from 10,000 feet, he's got 10 minutes until he's going to be dead or on his way to jail. So I told Earl, 'put the hook down and we'll see if I can give you a push.' And I told him 'all I want you to do is fly this thing as smooth as you've ever flown in your life.' Now of course with the engines flamed out, he has no hydraulic system, and it's totally a hydraulic airplane.

So we have what we call a ram air turbulent, a little small propeller that comes out the side of an airplane. It's got a little hydraulic generator and an electric generator in it. It will put out enough electricity to operate one radio. And where the hydraulic system ordinarily uses 3,000 pounds of pressure, this little system gives you 800 to 1,000 pounds. So his ability to fly the airplane is severely restricted. Yet he set it up in his glide and I've never seen such a rock solid airplane.

I eased in underneath him, and put the shoe on the tail hook (the device that catches the cable is called a shoe and is about this big around (spreads fingers about 4–5")). By this time, with no gas on the airplane, the airplane weighs about 30,000 pounds. The windshield on the F4 is about 1¼" thick glass, and is the only flat spot on the front of the airplane. So we put the tail hook on the front of the windshield. And very gently, no bumping or anything like that, and once we made contact, we eased the power up and sure enough we were able to push him.

Now, the tail hook is allowed to swivel side to side, so that if you land in a crosswind and take the cable it will straighten the airplane out and align it with the runway, etc. But it's held down firmly with a hydraulic accumulator, which keeps a lot of pressure on it and keeps it down so when you hit the runway, it won't skip over the wire. So we found that we could maintain contact for about 20 seconds at a time. And then we would slide off to the side and we'd have to back up a little bit, ease back in, get back into position, come back in with the power. But by doing this we were able to extend vertical speed to about 1,500 feet per minute, which meant that we were going to double his gliding distance and it looked like we were going to actually make it to the jungles in Laos. The jungle is a great place to hide. And that was what we were trying to do, to get these guys at least to the jungle where they had half a chance of evading until we could get some rescue people in and get them picked up.

It gets a little complicated at this point, because sometimes people say, 'what about yourselves.' Well, it's a horrible site to see a surfaced area missile make a direct hit on an airplane in formation with you that's less than 1,000 feet away, and not see anything come out of the fireball. You've just seen two of your friends vaporized and you can't stop the war. You can't say 'time out'—you have to keep going. And it also brings you to the realization that your life is no more important than the man in the other airplane. So there was no way that I could not stay with Earl. Because his life meant just as much to his family as mine and my back-seaters' did to ours. We managed to push the airplane 88 miles. We did reach the jungles of Laos. We all ejected. Earl and his back-seater both had broken backs from the ejection. The ejection seat, we've found, is really bad. But the Martin-Baker Company apparently wanted to make sure you got out of the airplane, so they put a big charge in it. We all had been warned that if you did eject that you probably would have compression fractures of the spine, but they weren't life threatening, they were painful, but you could keep moving. My back-seater was in great shape. He didn't get any damage from the ejection and neither did I. When I hit the ground—paratroopers here you'd have had a good laugh about my parachute landing—I went through a dead tree and it collapsed my parachute and allowed me to speed up pretty good before I hit the ground. I landed in a pile of rocks and my head impacted right between my feet. After we were rescued a few hours later and got back to Udorn, Thailand, another airbase, we were examined. I found out I had numerous cuts and bruises and two cracked vertebrae in my neck. It's amazing, I've always been pretty careful with my military records, but on the flight from Udorn back to Ubon, somehow that part of the record got lost. And my back-seater and I were back on the flying schedule a couple of days later. We had to go over there and sit around.

Earl and his back-seater went to the Philippines, spent about six weeks in the hospital, recovered, and came back. But it was funny. When we got back to our base, our whole squadron was there. It didn't seem like anybody was on the flying schedule. It seemed like almost everyone was there to welcome us home, popping champagne bottles. We gave them a debrief on what transpired. And as soon as the debriefing was over, the commander said 'I want to see you guys in my office.' That's when things started turning brown.

Apparently he had been asked by someone from our headquarters just what the hell I thought I was doing wasting a perfectly good F4 by trying to push another airplane out of North Vietnam. We tried to explain to them that I had received hits over the target and run out of gas. And it wouldn't have made a difference if I'd have gone straight to the tanker or hung around and circled the target; I would have run out of gas where I ran out of gas. But that never did filter up. Things don't filter upwards real well. They filter downward real good.

It was at that point that I realized that we weren't going to be allowed to win that war. And I think a lot of my friends felt the same way. It came over us rather slowly. We were going up there and losing people every day. And we weren't going to be allowed to win, because they wouldn't let us take out the right targets in the right fashion. And yet our ground troops in the South won the battles, we won the battles in the air over the North. And yet when a North

Vietnamese general was confronted with those facts about five years later, he said 'that's immaterial, we won the war.' Well, they didn't win the war. We gave them the war. Our politicians gave them the war.

One of the good results of the war was that a lot of our young lieutenants over there grew up to be the joint chiefs of staff. And they said 'never again will we commit troops without the ability to win the war.' And that was proved so well in Desert Storm—when the president tells the secretary of defense what he wants done, he told the chairman of the joint chiefs, and the chairman told his generals 'Call me when it's finished.' And it went just that way." (Pardo, 2002, 2003)

Story Notes

Colonel Bob Pardo remains steadfast in the welfare of his fellow airmen. When he discovered retired Lieutenant Colonel Earl Aman was stricken with Lou Gehrig's disease, he founded a foundation that raised the funds Earl needed for a wheelchair, a voice synthesizer, a computer, and even, with help from the Red River Valley Fighter Pilots Association (River Rats), a van. Earl drove that van until his death.

Pardo says, whether in war or in peace, "if one of us gets in trouble, everyone else gets together to help."

I met Bob through Mike Peters, who was the director at the Angel Fire Vietnam Memorial in Angel Fire, New Mexico, during 1994–1996 and then again at Celebrate Freedom, in Tennessee in 2003.

Chapter 19

The Sailor: Michael Peters

I've seen spices of the Orient.
I've seen Alaska's dancing lights and sailed her glacier Bays,
And I've sailed beneath the Southern Cross and dived reefs by day.
I've followed winds and searched world o're seven seas,
And never found the thing I sought.

—Pat Mendoza

There are not a lot of people—like Michael Peters—who can honestly say that they have witnessed the start of a war and watched the same war end nine years later.

Michael Peters was born on February 22, 1943, in River Rouge, Michigan. "I was born a blue baby, umbilical the cord was around my neck 3 times" (Peters). When Michael was delivered at his aunt's house, they thought he was stillborn. "It was more than 20 minutes before I started to cry" (Peters). Life was kind of difficult in Michigan, and in 1949, the family moved to Moose Pass, Alaska. Michael thought it was great there as a kid. He now realizes it wasn't as great for the adults because of all the snow. In 1957, when he was 14 years old, Michael's family relocated to Los Angeles, California.

What a switch—from a town of 125 to a city with 1,000,000 people was shocking to Michael. After 15 months, the family moved to the San Francisco Bay Area.

Mike remembers his first beating when he was four years old. His father was very abusive throughout his childhood years. To get away from home, his mother signed the papers for him to enter the military at the age of 17. On March 22, 1960, Michael immediately reported to recruit training in San Diego, California, and knew from the beginning that the Navy would be his home from then on. "I got good clear guidance during my first four years." Navy boot camp was the first hurdle in learning how to follow orders. "Marching in cadence seemed endless. Once a week the recruits were marched off to the base swimming pool" (Peters).

Swim time served not only as exercise. For the nonswimmers who joined, they would have to learn while they were in boot camp. Swimming lessons were required after their normal training. The culmination of all of this for the recruit was to jump off a 40-foot tower into the pool, then remove his pants and make floatation devices from them for "abandon ship" drills. The theory was that if recruits were successfully taught how to fight fires at sea, abandoning the ship would not be necessary.

Their credo was "knowing your job and the job of the guy next to you." If the chain of command was broken, the next in line was taught to take over. Each man knew how to complete the mission. They also knew their weapons as well as the gun manufacturers.

And then there was the ability to polish brass, what this had to do with combat is still a mystery, but it sure made things look all "pretty and shinny." By the time a navy recruit had graduated from boot camp, he had become a master brass polisher, whether he wanted to be or not. This was also true for mastering the "spit shinned" shoe. All uniforms would be immaculately pressed.

Upon Mike's graduation in 1964 from boot camp, he was ordered to serve aboard the USS *Harry E. Hubbard* (DD-748).

This WWII destroyer had a long distinguished history since her commissioning on July 22, 1944. *Harry E. Hubbard* resisted every imaginable enemy for nearly two months.

On May 11, 1945, after radar picket destroyers *Evans* and *Hugh W. Hadley* suffered heavy damage from 50 Japanese suicide planes the *Hubbard* was first to arrive. She traveled alongside *Evans*, giving fire-fighting help, as well as offering damage control and medical help. Similar aid was given to the destroyer *Barry* 24–25 May by the *Hubbard*. After shooting down two Japanese suicide planes, she brought *Barry* into Kerama Retto. According to the U.S. Naval records of September 2, 1945, the *Hubbard* and the *Evans* were the first destroyers to access the Russian-held port of Dairen, Manchuria. This was the same port the Commander Destroyer Squadron 64 negotiated the return from Mukden of some 1,500 prisoners. Many of these prisoners survived for years after the torture sustained during the infamous Bataan Death March. The crew on the *Hubbard* was astonished at how emaciated these 1,500 prisoners were when they came aboard; they were immediately transferred to a hospital ship in the Pacific. The *Hubbard* was decommissioned at the end of WWII, very briefly recommissioned during the Korean War, and the recommissioned again at the outbreak of the Vietnam War (USS *Harry E. Hubbard* (DD-748)).

Mike's first taste of combat was on the *Harry E. Hubbard*, which was like being thrown out of frying pan into the fire. Seventeen-year-old Mike Peters's baptism by fire was both exhilarating and frightening. When the North

Vietnamese torpedo boats attacked American destroyers that patrolled the Gulf of Tonkin, in August 1964, the *Harry E. Hubbard* came to the rescue. She happened to be screening *Ticonderoga* (CVA-14) near the South China Sea. The carrier group, made up of several U.S. ships including the *Hubbard*, struck back with hope of destroying North Vietnamese torpedo boats and any supporting forces.

Orders were heard: "General Quarters, General Quarters! All men man your battle stations!" The efficiency of the crew emptied the galley within seconds and the men of the USS *Harry E. Hubbard* got ready to fire the quad 40mm anti-aircraft gun, mounted aft on the bow. Mike Peters was in charge of a gun crew. He was the first loader and along with the second loader, their job was to hand a 24-pound, four round clip of ammunition to another man who would load the clip in the gun.

Following this event, the Navy Unit Commendation was awarded to the *Ticonderoga*, Secretary of the Navy Paul Nitze for demonstrating "the firm intent of the United States to maintain freedom of the seas and to take all necessary measures in defense of peace in Southeast Asia (Naval Historical Center).

Though this information was obtained after the fact, it appears that there was no North Vietnamese attack that night. U.S. authorities seemed convinced at the time that one had taken place. They reacted by sending planes from the carriers *Ticonderoga* and *Constellation* to hit North Vietnamese torpedo boat bases and fuel facilities (San Joaquin Valley Veterans). A few days later (on August 10, 1964), the U.S. Congress passed the Tonkin Gulf Resolution, which gave the government authorization for what eventually became a full-scale war in Southeast Asia (Tonkin Gulf Resolution).

Thus, began the Vietnam War.

In October 1964, Mike returned to Long Beach, California, as did the *Hubbard*. For the next year they prepared themselves for war. In October 1965, the *Hubbard* sailed with the carrier *Valley Forge*, heading for the coast of South Vietnam. Together they covered two marine amphibious landings, providing gunfire. Over the next months, they escorted two other carriers, the *Kitty Hawk* and *Hancock*, during their war campaign efforts in South China. The destroyer USS *Harry E. Hubbard* was used offshore of Danang, Vietnam, firing more than 1,000 rounds of 5-inch shells into the Viet Cong along the coast of South Vietnamese. On March 10, 1966, the *Hubbard* drew the America's attention when ABC Television aired scenes of her bombardments along the South Vietnamese coast.

Mike remembers USS *Hubbard* as a fine ship with an outstanding crew. During his time on the *Hubbard*, he advanced to first class GMG2 (E-5). *Hubbard* was his home for six years, until his transfer in 1970 to Norfolk, Virginia.

Mike fell in love and married, and wanted time with his new family. However, he was immediately transferred to the squadron going back to the

Mediterranean for about a year, spending time in different ports of call. Needless to say, his marriage did not work. Following the time in the Mediterranean, he was transferred to language school to learn Vietnamese fluently. He also attended the Navy Inshore Operation Training Center (NIOTC), where he also attended Survival School. He was then deployed back to Vietnam in February 1972, except this time he was placed in the middle of harm's way. Now an E-7 Chief Petty Officer, he was in charge of a Patrol Boat River (PBR) squadron. Mike reported in country April Fools' Day, 1972 and was there until February 1973.

Anyone who has ever seen the rivers in Vietnam understands the nickname of "Brown Water Navy." The rivers, rice paddies, and mud were in the same brown color. The job of the PBRs was to patrol the Mekong River and its tributaries and cut off the enemy supply routes. Most of their patrols were at night, and the night belonged to "Charlie," the Viet Cong.

Patrolling the rivers was extremely hazardous duty. The rivers were audible in the land of "midnight screams." Many times, PBRs were ambushed from the riverbanks, and those 31-foot fiberglass boats didn't stop bullets! A tremendous amount of time was spent pulling alongside sampans and junks, or other boats on the river, searching them for contraband. Searchers had to be careful because "Charlie" was ingenious in the ways he could kill you. Sometimes a bamboo viper was placed in a sampan, with its tail tacked down, where a searching hand might reach. If bitten, a man's life expectancy decreased to about 15 minutes. Often, when searchers pulled up to a boat, "Charlie" would lob a "Chicom," a Chinese communist-made grenade, onto the PBR. There were all kinds of ways to die in this beautiful, lethal land.

Death was ever present in life along the river. On more than one occasion, there were dog heads floating in the water near villages that grew up out of the Mekong Delta's vegetation. The rest of the dogs' body was part of the local cuisine.

During the warm season, you would cool down any way you could, even if it meant getting wet. As if giving heed to some strange jungle rutting call, Mike Peters and the seven other members of the two PBR crews appeared naked from their hooches (slang for a hut) and ran into the rain with bars of soap, and began taking their long awaited showers. The sight of these eight naked men baying at the delta's monsoons while lathering their bodies caused a local mamma-san to run shrieking, "Dinky dow! Bou coup dinky dow!" as she ran for her life. Mike laughed to himself as he thought of the old woman's words: "Dinky dow"—crazy. Yes, they were all a little bit crazy.

There was an old joke that was told in country, you never prayed for rain because once a monsoon arrived it never stopped and you never wanted to ever see rain again.

During his time with the PBRs, Mike was stationed at logistic support base (LSB), Binh Thuy. He was an advisor to the weapons shop as well as an operational advisor to many boats. As the weapons advisor his primary duties were to install MK 19 MOD1 grenade launchers. He was also senior enlisted for several months. As stated by Richard Nixon, in 1973, the *cease-fire agreement* "brings peace with honor in Vietnam and Southeast Asia." The document was signed in Paris by Henry Kissinger and Le Duc Tho. The agreement went into effect on January 28. Binh Thuy was the last base to close in the Mekong Delta in 1973, and Mike Peters was there until the end. As they departed, all of the remaining equipment was signed over to State Department representatives.

Mike retired as master chief petty officer after 18 years' service to the United States.

Story Notes

I met Mike Peters around 1995, when he had just become the director of the Vietnam Veterans Memorial in Angel Fire, New Mexico; and I took two busloads of Denver students to visit the Memorial, as I did every year. We quickly became friends when we discovered that both of us did time with PBRs in Vietnam, and we have remained friends since that time. Mike Peters finished his military career in Millington, Tennessee, where he was the training programmer for all gunners in the Navy. He retired in 1980 at the rank of E-9, the highest rank he could receive as an enlisted man. He wanted to return to sea, but the Navy didn't have any duty for him there.

I included the full history of the USS Harry E. Hubbard because during the years I have known Mike Peters, I was able to introduce him to Sam Antonio and Tony Reyna, who were both POWs in Mukden Prison and involved in the Bataan Death March. Mike then researched the navy logs for Sam and Tony of the Harry E. Hubbard, since the ship had been part of all of their history.

I've also had the opportunity to meet Mike's sister Kathleen, who regards her brother Mike highly. Mike also has one other sister, Karen, and a brother.

Chapter 20

Immigrant Soldier: Cecilia Vivar

*When an opportunity arises, take a chance and pursue it. There are numer-
ous says to support the U.S. troops. What started as an opportunity to
correspond and become a pen pal, begat the start of a long-time friendship.
Ask yourself, "what can I do to help our troups?" This is a story from such
a pen pal.*

For a thousand years, people have yearned to find out what is on the other
side of the mountain. It takes courage to uproot your family and sever old
friendships. But it is the dream of every parent to build a better life for their
children.

Unforeseen circumstances brought about changes for Silvano Vivar (age 17)
and his young wife Matilde Cabrera (age 16). Matilde gave birth to a baby
girl in January 1983. Christened Cecilia Vivar, she was born in the state of Oaxaca, Mexico, located about 100 miles south of Mexico City. A year later, a little
boy was born.

Squalor and living conditions plagued Cecilia's family life. If they were
going to survive, her parents decided that the best thing to do was to leave the
state of Oaxaca. Cecilia's father and everyone else in their town were talking
about the "land of opportunities" (Ortega).

Cecilia's parents gathered enough money to pay for a bus to take their
family from their home state to Baja California, Mexico. Once in Baja, her
parents worked a few more months to pay off a Coyote—a smuggler— to bring
them to America. Cecilia was four and her brother was three. After they crossed
the border, a bus took the family from San Ysidro, California, to Santa Maria,
California. This is where her family ended up residing permanently.

Some of Cecilia's memories are about the one-bedroom apartment her
family quickly found to live in with another family, and their working conditions.

"There were seven of us living in very tight conditions" (Vivar). They also found work in the fields picking strawberries and doing a lot of field labor for a few hundred dollars a week, enough to pay for food and shelter. Cecilia and her brother would sometimes go to work with her parents because there was nowhere else her parents could leave them due to lack of money for day care. She and her brother would be in the field from sunrise to sunset. She doesn't remember her parents having too much time to play with them, because they were too tired to even move.

In 1988, her mom had a second boy, Jesus. That was the year when Cecilia started elementary school. She was in a schoolroom where she didn't even understand what the teachers said, because she didn't know the language. For that reason, she was placed in English second language (ESL) classes. Learning English was a challenge, because in class she was being taught one language and at home all she heard was a different one. It took more than four years of ESL classes before Cecilia was finally placed in a regular English class. Anything she learned, she would teach her younger brothers so they could learn as well. Her first brother had a hard time just like her with his English barriers. But her second brother, Jesus, learned faster, because she would help him out as much as she could. During her time out of school, she was also helping her mother out with laundry, cooking, and cleaning. She really didn't have much free time to be a child and play outside with other children. Her mother gave birth to two more boys, and Cecilia was their second mom—always helping her mother out in every way she could.

Cecilia was too young to understand the severity of her legal situation back then. But her parents quickly processed their paperwork through their employer, and they were able to become legal U.S. residents through this amnesty. Fate intervened when President George W. Bush granted amnesty for illegal aliens. Cecilia remembered

> This amnesty forgave their act of illegal immigration and implicitly forgave other related illegal acts such as driving and working using false documents. The result of an amnesty is that large numbers of foreigners who illegally gained entry into the United States were rewarded with legal status.

Ten years later, Cecilia became a U.S. citizen.

Statistics show that Hispanics have low levels of education beyond high school compared with Anglos. However, according to the U.S. Census Bureau, the Hispanic population is certainly showing dramatic improvement and attaining higher education levels (U.S. Census).

Cecilia did not want to be another statistic. She graduated from high school in the summer of 2001, and moved out of her parents' home to pursue her American dream of a higher education. She moved two hours south of Santa Maria to attend ITT-Technical Institute. Her goal was to continue her schooling, without a gap between schools. She chose to pursue a degree in computer drafting, and worked at a gas station to pay for her expenses during college. Cecilia purchased her first car, got her driver's license, and her very first credit card.

At the start of Cecilia's second quarter of college on September 11, 2001, terrorists attacked the Pentagon and World Trade Center. Cecilia immediately knew exactly how she was going to serve her country to pay it back for everything it had offered to her and her family. She decided to join the U.S. Navy. Although she considered dropping out of her program to join the military; that would have required her to pay a lot of money for the classes she had already taken. Therefore, she decided to finish college and then sign a contract with the military as soon as she graduated from college. All of her struggles paid off.

In September 2003, Cecilia completed a two-year program with ITT-Technical Institute, earning an associate's degree in computer drafting and design.

Cecilia remembers it well,

It was October 27, 2007 at about 2000 hours. I was sitting in my living room watching "Dora the Explorer" with my daughter two year old Michelle when I received a phone call from Plans, Operations and Medical Intelligence (POMI) Office in San Diego, California.

The POMI Office is responsible for ensuring that military staff members are fully medically ready for deployment as well as selecting a qualifying billet for the deploying member.

The POMI Office informed me that I had been selected for a tour of duty in Baghdad, Iraq. My orders stated that I would report no later the than 26 November 2007 at Navy Mobilization Processing Site (NMPS) for initial check in and a week later head out to Fort Bliss, Texas for Counter, Rocket, Artillery and Mortar (C-RAM) Operator training. The C-RAM helps protects US forces and coalition troops against mortars and rockets fired by insurgents, therefore C-RAM training was a very important part of the mission. My orders had me scheduled to be in training for 20 weeks before deploying to Iraq for the mission. Training was a bunch of 'hurry up and wait' wasted time for those of us with families and loved ones who were waiting for us back at home. Those four and a half months could have easily been crunched down to four weeks.

My husband and daughter stayed in touch with me using Skype and Yahoo Messenger, software applications that allows users to make voice calls and chats over the Internet. Skype and Yahoo Messenger were life savers.

Cecilia's training was rigorous. During this time, she acquired basic knowledge of the following:

- M16 familiarization and qualification
- Crew-served weapons (M2 and MK 19 familiarization and qualification)
- Short-range and advanced-range marksmanship
- Suicide awareness/combat stress training
- Single channel ground and airborne radio system (SINCGARS) training
- Force protection, law of war, and return on expectations ROE training
- Movement training
- Army Humvee driving training (HMMWV)
- Land navigation training land defense advanced GPS receiver (PLGR/ DAGR)
- Insurgent methods training improvised explosive devices (IMT IED) training
- Combat lifesaver training
- Dismounted improvised explosive devices (IED) training
- COIN training
- Countered-improvised explosive device tactics, techniques, and procedures (CIED-TTP) training
- Combat defense patrol training
- Close quarters combat/movement over urban terrain (MOUT)
- Convoy operations to include battle drills and live fire exercises.

Once the training was completed, her unit was ready for their mission. Everyone was excited to go to Iraq and see what new experiences they were going to face. While boarding the plane that was taking them to their destination, Cecilia recalls praying that everything should go well. The plane made several stops to gas up. Some of those sites included Canada, Germany, Iceland, and other places. Their boots set on ground Wednesday, April 23, 2008. It was in Camp Victory in Baghdad, Iraq. This is where Cecilia would spend the next six months with her team of 62 members. It took several weeks for her to get use to the weather, the time, and the food. It was culture shock.

I really didn't know what exactly to expect, but when I finally saw with my own eyes the difference, I quickly learned to value everything at home much more. For example, the fact that the Soldiers, Sailors, Marines and Airmen on base were RESTRICTED to certain areas on the camp, and had little to no choices as far as what to do and where to go. This made the deployment feel extensive and dreary. I was in Iraq for three months when it finally hit me, I just want to go home and be with my family. At the same time, I knew I was there supporting my country and quickly realized that what I was doing wasn't in vain, but it was my part in support of this great nation's fight for freedom.

Standing watch (being at her assigned station) was Cecilia's main mission. As a C-RAM operator, she was at the mount by 2345 until 1200 the next day. Her watches lasted 12 hours long, and that's all she did—stand watch. If something happened, she was prepared to aim and shoot at the enemy. This meant releasing the button to fire against any mortars, rockets, and artillery. She had the opportunity to shoot once. On Saturday, July 26, 2008,

> I was standing watch at about 0845; I was just about to have breakfast, when all I saw was a red screen. The C-RAM sensors had detected a target. Once I knew the target had been detected, the audio and visual alarms began to sound. My heart began racing 100mph. I knew I would see the mortar round on my screen and that I would be the one to destroy it. Since the C-RAM predicts the mortar's path prioritizes the target, I was able to push the button and defeat the round while still in the air. All this took place within seconds. (Vivar)

The screen on the C-RAM showed how the enemy missile was destroyed in a million pieces. She says one of the best feelings she had while deployed was *"Knowing that I was fighting the enemy."*

Cecilia, like of the most GIs, suffered from homesickness. To make matters worse, Cecilia knew she would not see her husband, James, or daughter, Michelle, until the tour of duty at was over. Her active military tour was five and a half years long. She was discharged on May 2, 2009.

Cecilia, James, and Michelle reside in Southern California, where Cecilia is working full time. She has completed her bachelor's degree in business administration, specializing in Human Resource Management, and is working with the Navy Reserves. James, her husband, is a full-time police officer.

Today, Cecilia believes that joining the military was the best decision she ever made. All the benefits (tuition assistance, free medical and dental, housing, sustenance, and much more) could not compare to any other benefits other jobs could offer. But, the main reason she joined the military was to serve her country. She went on to say,

> *I cannot be more proud to say that I am a US citizen fighting for my country, and I have alliance with no other one.*

Story Notes

My wife, Dona, and I met Cecilia through an online organization helping to connect American citizens with soldiers. We began corresponding with her while she was in Iraq, to help her have a link to home. Her story about being an immigrant soldier truly captured my interest, because such stories are not often publicized. She lives in California, where her husband is a policeman, and we have never met in person. But we have maintained correspondence after her return. Cecilia is still on Active Reserve in California. In March 2013, Cecilia returned to active duty and is serving a tour of duty in Afghanistan. She will work on her MBA online during her downtime there. Dona and Cecilia continue to email during her time in Afghanistan.

Sources

Chapter 1—"The Devil Himself Could Not Catch Him"— Francis Marion

Bass, Robert D. *Swamp Fox: The Life and Campaigns of General Francis Marion*. New York: Holt, 1959.

Patriot Resource website: http://www.patriotshistoryusa.com/teaching-materials/bonus-materials/american-heroes-francis-marion/ [accessed 12/18/13].

South Carolina Historical Society Archives: Unpublished correspondences of Francis Marion, Peter Horry, and Lord Cornwallis Jenkins, James Experience, "Labours and Sufferings," 1842.

Wilcox, Clark (oral historian and resident of Murrell's Inlet, South Carolina). Video interview with the author, 1980.

Chapter 2—The Voodoo Queen and the Pirate—Marie Leveau and Jean Lafitte

"The Battle of New Orleans, 1815," Eyewitness to History website: http://www.eyewitnesstohistory.com/battleofneworleans.htm [accessed 8/28/13].

Fandrich, Ina J. *The Mysterious Voodoo Queen, Marie Laveaux: A Study of Powerful Female Leadership in Nineteenth Century New Orleans (Studies in African American History and Culture*. New York: Routledge Publishing Company, 2005.

"Marie Catherine Laveau: Voodoo Queen of New Orleans (September 10, 1801–June 15, 1881)," Strange History website: http://www.strangehistory.org/cms/index.php/home/17-marie-catherine-laveau-voodoo-queen-of-new-orleans-september-10-1801-june-15-1881 [accessed 8/28/13].

Ramsay, Jack C., Jr. *Jean Lafitte: Prince of Pirates*. Austin, TX: Eakin Press, 1996.

Subaltern, Gleig. "A Contemporary Account of the Battle of New Orleans by a Soldier in the Rank." *Louisiana Historical Quarterly,* January 9, 1926, pp. 11–15.

Chapter 3—For God? Or for Country?—John Riley and the San Patricios of the Mexican War

American Heritage website: http://www.americanheritage.com/content/tragic-story-san-patricio-battalion [accessed 8/28/13].

Anderson, Gary Clayton. *Little Crow: Spokesman for the Sioux*. Minnesota Historical Society Press, 1986.

Digital History website: http://www.digitalhistory.uh.edu/historyonline/irish_potato_famine.cfm [accessed 1/9/2014].

"The Irish in America," Greystone Communications A&E Network, 1995.

Stevens, Peter. *The Rogue's March: John Riley and the St. Patrick's Battalion, 1846–48 (The Warriors)*. Virginia: Potomac Books, 2005.

The Struggle website: http://www.struggle.ws/mexico/img/more_san_ps.html [accessed 8/28/13].

Chapter 4—It All Started in His Front Yard—Wilmer McClean

Davis, Burke. *To Appomattox: Nine April Days 1865*. Durham, NC: Eastern Acorn Press, 1959.

Davis, Burke. *Sherman's March*. New York: Random House, 1980.

"The First Battle of Bull Run, 1861, Eye Witness to History," Eyewitness to History website: www.eyewitnesstohistory.com (2004) [accessed 8/28/13].

Freeman, Douglas Southall. *R. E. Lee: A Biography*. Volume IV. New York: Charles Scribner' Sons, 1936.

Grant, Ulysses Simpson. *Personal Memoirs of U.S. Grant* (originally published by Mark Twain in 1885). New York: Da Capo Press, 1952.

Schreadley, R. L. "Sharpsburg/Antietam: Bloodiest Day in American History." *The Post and Courier* website: http://www.postandcourier.com/article/20070917/ARCHIVES/309179980 (2012).

Ward, Geoffrey C. Ward and Kenneth Burns. *The Civil War : The Complete Text of the Bestselling Narrative History of the Civil War.* Vintage, 1994.

Ward, Jeffery and Burns. *The Civil War.* New York: Random House, 1992.

White River Valley Historical Quarterly, Volume 3, Issue 7, Spring 1969. www.thelibrary.org/lochist/periodicals/wrv/v3/n7/Sp69g.htm [accessed 8/28/13].

Chapter 5—To Serve Proud and Free—Isaiah Mays

Arlington National Cemetery website: http://www.arlingtoncemetery.mil/ [accessed 9/1/13].

Ball, Larry. *Ambush at Bloody Run.* Arizona State Historic Society, 2000.

The Missing Americans Project official website: http://missingamericans.ning.com/ [accessed 12/18/13].

Remington, Fredric. "A Scout with the Buffalo Soldiers." *The Century; A Popular Quarterly.* Volume 37, Issue 6, April 1889.

Chapter 6—To Walk Softly and Carry a Big Stick—Theodore Roosevelt

Congressional Medal of Honor Society website: http://www.cmohs.org/recipient-detail/2178/roosevelt-theodore.php [accessed 9/1/13].

Jeffers, H. Paul. *Colonel Roosevelt: Theodore Roosevelt Goes to War, 1897–1898.* New York: John Wiley & Sons, 1996.

Morris, Edmund. *Colonel Roosevelt.* New York: Random House, 2010.

Morris, Edmund. *The Rise of Theodore Roosevelt.* New York: Coward, McCann & Geoghegan, 1979.

Chapter 7—To Vanish in the Morning—Blanche Hennebery and George MacCrae

Byrd, Michael J. *The Town That Died.* London: Souvenir Press, 1962.

Maritime Museum of the Atlantic website: http://museum.gov.ns.ca/mma/AtoZ/halexpl.html [accessed 9/1/13].

McCrae, George (WWII Marine Corps Raider veteran and blast survivor). Personal interview with the author, 2004.

Sigona, Suzanne (granddaughter of Blanche Hennebery). Personal interview with the author, 1994.

Chapter 8—We Laid Aside the Citizen—Joe Angelo and the Veteran's Bonus March

D'Este, Carlo. *Patton: A Genius for War*. New York: Harper Collins Publishers, 1996.

George S. Patton, Jr. official website: www.general.patton.com.

Home of Heroes website: http://www.homeofheroes.com/ [accessed 9/1/13].

Library of Congress website: http://www.americaslibrary.gov/aa/patton/aa_patton_bonus_1.html [accessed 9/1/13].

PBS. The American Experience website: http://www.pbs.org/wgbh/amex/macarthur/peopleevents/pandeAMEX89.html [accessed 9/1/13].

Zezima, Michael. *50 American Revolutions You're Not Supposed to Know: Reclaiming American Patriotism*. Oklahoma: Disinformation Books, 2005.

Chapter 9—The Fighting Quaker—Smedley Darlington Butler

Archer, Jules. *Plot to Seize the White House: The Shocking True Story of the Conspiracy to Overthrow FDR*. New York: Skyhorse Publishing, 2007.

Butler Smedley D. *War Is a Racket: The Antiwar Classic by America's Most Decorated Hero*. New York: New York Round Table Press, Inc., 1935 (Reprinted in 2003 by Feral House).

Medal of Honor Citations official website: http://www.history.army.mil/moh.html [accessed 9/1/13].

U.S. House. Committee on Un-American Activities. Investigation of Nazi Propaganda Activities and Investigation of Certain Other Propaganda Activities: Public Hearings before the Special, House of Representatives, Seventy-third Congress, Second Session, at Washington, DC, December 29, 1934. Hearings No. 73-D.C.-6, Part 1.

The White House Coup. BBC documentary, 2007. Mike Thomson. With readings by Peter Marinker and Kerry Shale. Produced by Philip Sellers.

Chapter 10—A Miracle in the Trenches—Robert Hulse

"The Christmas Truce of 1914." http://www.firstworldwar.com/features/christ mastruce.htm [accessed 9/2/13].

"The Great War." NBC News Productions, 1956. Written by Henry Salomon with Richard Hanser; narrated by Alexander Scourby.

http://www.nytimes.com/2005/12/25/weekinreview/25word.ready.html? pagewanted=all&_r=0 [accessed 9/2/13].

http://www.1914-1918.net/truce.htm [accessed 9/2/13].

Lee, Robert quote. http://ushistorysite.com/robert_e_lee_quotes.php [accessed 9/2/13].

MacCrae, John. *In Flander's Fields and Other Poems*. New York: Thomas Y. Crowell Co., 1919.

MacCrae, Lieutenant Colonel John. Arlington National Cemetery website: http://www.arlingtoncemetery.net/flanders.htm [accessed 9/2/13].

PBS California. WGBII, The American Experience. "Timeline: Influenza across America in 1918." http.//www.pbs.org/wgbh/amex/influenza/time line/index.html [accessed 9/2/13].

Tennessee State Parks website: http://www.tn.gov/environment/parks/SgtYork/ [accessed 9/2/13].

Chapter 11—The Last Acoma—Sam Antonio

Antonio, Sam. Personal interviews with the author, 1984–2004.

Camp O'Donnell Provost Report. November 19, 1945. http://www.mansell .com/pow_resources/camplists/philippines/odonnell/provost_rpt.html [accessed 9/2/13].

Mendoza, Patrick. *Extraordinary People in Extraordinary Times: Heroes, Sheroes, and Villains*. Englewood, CO: Libraries Unlimited, 1999.

Moore, Christopher. *Fighting for America: Black Soldiers—Unsung Heroes of WWII*. New York: One World/Ballantine, 2004.

Chapter 12—The First Son and the Second Marines—James Roosevelt and Carlson's Raiders

Bauml, Ray (2nd Marine Raiders Company A). Personal interviews with the author, 2000–2010.

Carlson, Colonel Evans. Personal correspondence with Carolyn Nodland. Supplied by Georgi Annie Nodland Petrow, sister of Private Franklin "Bud" Nodland. Now on file at the Marine Corps Raiders Museum in Quantico, VA United States Marine Corps Raiders Association website: http://www .usmarineraiders.org [accessed 1/9/2014].

"Evans Fortyce Carlson, Brigadier General United States Marine Corps," Arlington National Cemetery website: http://www.arlingtoncemetery.net/ efcarlson.htm [accessed 1/9/2014].

"James Roosevelt Dies at 83; Last Surviving Child of Ex-President," *Los Angeles Times* website: http://articles.latimes.com/1991-08-14/news/ mn-469_1_james-roosevelt [accessed 12/18/13].

Military Times. "Hall of Valor." http://projects.militarytimes.com/citations-med als-awards/recipient.php?recipientid=8339 [accessed 12/18/13].

Nodland, Franklin M. U.S. Marine Corp. Personal Letters to Home during WWII, January 1942–July 1942.

Petrow, Annie. Interviews between Nodland's sister and author, 2002–2009.

Roosevelt, James with Bill Libby. *My Parents: A Differing View.* Chicago, IL: Playboy Press, 1976.

U.S. Marine Raider Association and Foundation. Carlson's eulogy. www .usmarineraiders.org/makin.html [accessed 9/2/13].

Chapter 13—From the Navy Hymn to Davy Jones' Locker— Gordon Skinner

CNIC Naval Weapons Yorktown website: http://www.cnic.navy.mil/Yorktown/ index.htm [accessed 9/2/13].

NavSource Online: USS *Yorktown* Aircraft Carrier Photo Archive. http://www .navsource.org/archives/02/10.htm [accessed 9/2/13].

Skinner, Gordon. Personal interviews with the author, 2004.

USS *Sterlet* website: http://www.usssterlet.com [accessed 9/2/13].

Chapter 14—In the Shadow of Giants—Ray Bauml

Bauml, Lillian. Personal interviews with the author, 2000–2010.

Bauml, Raymond. Diary of Raymond Bauml (unpublished).

Bauml, Raymond. Personal interviews with the author, 2000–2010.

Marine Corps Raiders Museum website: http://www.usmarineraiders.org/muse
umhistory.html [accessed 9/7/13].

Chapter 15—No Greater Love—Bryant Womack

Bynum, William B. *The Heritage of Rutherford County North Carolina, Vol. I.*
Winston-Salem, NC: Genealogical Society of Old Tryon County Incorporated in cooperation with the History Division, Hunter Publishing Company, 1984.

The King James Bible. Cleveland, OH: World Publishing Co, 1945.

Kupperson, Sam (sergeant). Personal interviews with the author, 1978.

"US Army Center of Military History," U.S. Military Files website: http://www
.history.army.mil [accessed 9/7/13].

Womack, George. Personal interviews of Bryan Womack's nephew by the
author, 1978–2010.

Chapter 16—A Nurse's Story—Jonita Ruth Bonham

Bonham, Jonita Ruth, Personal letters, 1950.

Bovcé, Renee. Personal interview of daughter of Jonita Ruth Bonham, 1994.

Flight Nurse. Directed by Alan La May. USA: Republic Pictures. 1954.

Mendoza, Patrick. *Extraordinary People in Extraordinary Times: Heroes, Sheroes, and Villains.* Englewood, CO: Libraries Unlimited, 1999.

Chapter 17—The Day "Doc" Goss Became a Nurse—
Jim Goss

Department of the Army. "Applied Participation in Vietnam." http://www.his
tory.army.mil/books/Vietnam/allied/ [accessed 1/9/14].

Department of the Army. "Mountain Combat in Vietnam." http://www.history
.army.mil/books/Vietnam/mounted/ [accessed 1/9/14].

Goss, Jim. Personal interviews with the author, 1986–2011.

History Channel. http://www.history.com/topics/vietnam-war [accessed 1/9/14].

Naval Historical Center. http://www.history.navy.mil/danfs/h3/harry_e_hub
bard.htm [accessed 1/9/14].

Peters, Michael. Personal interviews with the author, 1994–2011.

San Joaquin Valley Veterans. http://www.sjvv.org/articles/spotlight1/tonkin gulf.html [accessed 9/11/13].

Tonkin Gulf Resolution. http://www.ourdocuments.gov/doc.php?flash=true& doc=98 [accessed 9/11/13].

"Vietnam Marines Da Nang Landing." YouTube. http://www.youtube.com/ watch?v=st5ax71ZCHg [accessed 9/7/13].

Chapter 18—Pardo's Push—Bob Pardo

Airforce-Magazine.com: online journal of the Air Force Association. "Pardo's Push." http://www.airforcemag.com/MagazineArchive/Pages/1996/Octo ber%201996/1096valor.aspx [accessed 12/18/13].

Pardo, Bob. Interview with the author in Pigeon Ford, TN, 2002.

Pardo, Bob. Public appearance, Celebrate Freedom, TN, 2003.

"Pardo's Push: An Incredible Feat of Airmanship." http://www.historynet.com/ pardos-push-an-incredible-feat-of-airmanship.htm [accessed 9/2013].

"Pardo's Push: McDonnell F4 Phantom." http://www.youtube.com/embed/ RRNbcPS3A9c?feature=player_detailpage [accessed 9/2013].

Chapter 19—The Sailor—Michael Peters

Amphibious Photo Archive USS *Hubbard*. http://www.navsource.org/ archives/10/04/04053.htm.

Dictionary of American Naval Fighting Ships website: http://www.hazegray .org/danfs/

Naval History and Heritage, USS *Harry Hubbard*. http://www.history.navy.mil/ danfs/h8/hubbard.htm

Peters, Michael. Personal interviews with author, 1995–2012.

The Vietnam Center and Archive website: http://www.vietnam.ttu.edu/resources/

Chapter 20—Immigrant Soldier—Cecilia Vivar

Ortega, Roberto Garcia. *El noreste de Mexico y Texas: asimetrias y convergen- cias territoriales en las relaciones tranfronterizas.* Colegio de la Frontera Norte. 2009. Tijuana, Baja California, Mexico.

US Census, "Table 229. Educational Attainment by Race and Hispanic Origin." http://www.census.gov/compendia/statab/2012/tables/12s0229.pdf.

Vivar, Cecilia. Telephone interviews with author, 2010–2011.

Index

Acoma people, 75–76
Afghanistan War. *See* Iraq and
 Afghanistan Wars
African Americans: in Civil War,
 34; 54th Massachusetts Regi-
 ment, 34; racial discrimination
 against, 35; in Revolutionary
 War, 36; Vietnam War and,
 139. *See also* Buffalo Soldiers;
 Slavery
Agnew, Art, 22
Aircraft carriers, 102. *See also spe-*
 cific carriers
The Alamo, 20
Alger, Russell, 42–43
Aman, Earl, 142–46
Angelo, Joe, 51–57; Patton and,
 55–56
Antiwar protests, Vietnam, 137
Antonio, Sam, 75–83; "Battling Bas-
 tards of Bataan" and, 75, 79;
 Bronze Star awarded to, 83; as
 POW, 79–82; in WWII, 77–79
Argonaut (submarine), 112–13;
 Makin Island raid and, 116

Army, U.S.: African Americans in,
 34; ex-slaves in, 35; Irish deser
 tions from, 19 20; Irish in, 18
Army Air Corps, 127
Arnold, Benedict, 17
Attucks, Crispus, 36

Banzai attacks, 114, 118
Bataan Death March, 78–79
Bataan Peninsula, Philippines,
 78–79
Battle of Buena Vista, 20
Battle of Bull Run, 28–29
Battle of Camden, 6
Battle of Convent Churubusco, 21
Battle of Coral Sea, 97–98
Battle of Cowpens, 7
Battle of Midway, 98–99; Carlson's
 Raiders and, 111
Battle of New Orleans, 9–14; British
 and, 12–13; Jackson, A., and,
 11–14; Lafitte and, 13; Leveau
 and, 13
Battle of Shiloh, 28–29
Battle of Ypres, 73

"Battling Bastards of Bataan," 75, 79
Bauml, Ray, 88–89, 90–91, 105–19;
    Battle of Midway and, 111;
    Carlson's Raiders and, 109–12;
    Makin Island raid, 112–17;
    Marine Corps boot camp,
    107–9
Beauregard, P.T.G., 27; Shiloh and,
    29
Beckwourth, James Pierson, 34–35
BIA. *See* Bureau of Indian Affairs
Big business in war, 65–66
Binh Thuy, Vietnam, 153
Blue Jacket's Manual (U.S. Navy),
    95
Bonham, Jonita Ruth: in Army Air
    Corps, 127; C-54 crash and,
    130–32; DFC awarded to, 132;
    in Korean War, 127–33
Bonus Expeditionary Force, 54
Bougainville, Solomon Islands,
    91–92
Boveé, Clifford, 128, 133
Boxer Rebellion, 61
Branch, John L., 26
Breed's Hill, 1
British: Battle of New Orleans and,
    12–13; Christmas Truce in
    1914, 71–74; Revolutionary
    War and, 4; War of 1812 and, 9
Brown, Benjamin, 37–38
Brown, John, 25
Brown, Vera, 130
"Brown Mountain Lights," 123
"Brown Water Navy," 152
Buffalo Soldiers, 33; in Indian Wars,
    35–36; racial discrimination
    against, 38; 24th Infantry Reg-
    iment, 35; in Western United
    States, 36
Buffalo Soldiers Motorcycle Club,
    39–40

Bunker Hill, 1
Bureau of Indian Affairs (BIA), 76
Burgoyne, John, 6
Burn, Harry, 53
Bush, George W., 156
Butaritari island, 106–7; people of,
    115
Butler, Smedley Darlington, 59–67;
    big business in war and, 65–66;
    as director of Public Safety for
    the City of Philadelphia, 65;
    in Haitian rebellion, 61–62; in
    Marine Corps, 59–65; Medals
    of Honor awarded to, 62–64;
    Pershing and, 63; in Philippine
    American War, 60–61; plot to
    overthrow Roosevelt, F., and,
    66–67; retirement of, 65; in
    Spanish American War, 60; in
    WWI, 63–64

Caco rebels, Haiti, 61–62
Canada: Halifax Disaster, 45–50; in
    WWI, 45
Capone, Al, 53, 106
Carlson, Evan F., 85, 87–92; Makin
    Island raid, 88–89
Carlson's Raiders, 85–92; Battle
    of Midway and, 111; Bauml
    and, 109–12; in Bougainville
    battle, 91–92; in Guadalcanal,
    91; "Long Patrol," 118; Makin
    Island raid, 88–89, 112–17; in
    New Hebrides Islands, 89–90; at
    Pearl Harbor, 112; Roosevelt, F.,
    and, 87–88; Roosevelt, J., and,
    87–88; rubber boat training,
    110, 112–14; termination of,
    91–92; three-man fire teams, 91;
    training, 109–10. *See also* Carl-
    son, Evan F.; Roosevelt, James
Catholicism, 18–19

Chandler, William Astor, 42
"Charlie," 152
Cherokee War, 2–3
"Chicom," 152
China, 61
Christmas Truce in 1914, 71–74
Civil War: African Americans in,
    34; Battle of Bull Run, 28–29;
    Lee's surrender to Grant and,
    30; McLean and, 25–31; Shiloh
    and, 28–29; South Carolina
    and, 26; Southern states after,
    34; states' succession and, 26;
    Virginia and, 26–27
Clinton, William, 43
Cold War, 124
Communism, 124; Vietnamese, 136
Confederate States of America, 26
Constellation (carrier), 152
Constitutional Amendments: Four-
    teenth, 34; Nineteenth, 52–53
Cornwallis, Charles, 7
Counter, Rocket, Artillery and Mor-
    tar (C-RAM) operator, 157
C-RAM operator. See Counter,
    Rocket, Artillery and Mortar
    Operator
Cuba, 42
Custer, George Armstrong, 30, 35
Czechoslovakia, 111–12

"Davey Jones' Locker," 99
Davis, Jefferson, 18
Depth charge attacks, 100–101
Desertion in Mexican War, 19–20, 22
Desert Storm, 147
Dewey, George, 42
Distinguished Flying Cross (DFC),
    132

Eisenhower, Dwight D., 55
Ellwood Plantation, Virginia, 64

Emancipation Proclamation, 33–34
England, 17–18
Enola Gay, 102

F4 airplanes, 142, 144–45
F105 airplanes, 142
54th Massachusetts Regiment, 34
Fourteenth Amendment, 34
French and Indian War, 2

Gaston, Daniel, 115
Gates, Horatio, 5–7
Germany: Christmas Truce in 1914,
    71–74; submarine warfare,
    45–46
Geronimo, 37
Gilbert Islands. See Makin Island
    raid
Goss, Jim, 135–40; as Hospital
    Corpsman, 138
Grant, Ulysses Simpson, 18; Lee
    and, 30; Shiloh and, 28–29
Great Depression, 53, 106–7
Great Potato Famine of 1845, 17
Green Dragoons, 4
Greene, Nathanial, 7
Gross, Samuel, 62
Guadalcanal, 91, 118
Guerrilla-type warfare, 3, 87
Gulf of Tonkin, 136–37, 150–51

Haitian rebellion, 61–62
Halifax Disaster, 45–50; blizzard
    and, 49; Mont Blanc explosion,
    46–48; rescue efforts, 48
Hancock (carrier), 151
Hedger, Ruben, 110
Hemingway, Ernest, 71
Henneberry, Blanche, 46–47
Heydrich, Reinhard, 111–12
Hiroshima, Japan, 102
Hispanics, 156–57

Hitler, Adolf, 106
Hokka Maru (freighter), 81
Hood, John B., 29
Hoover, Herbert, 54
Hooverville, 54
Hospital Corpsman School, 138
Houston, Sam, 20
Hulse, Robert, 69–74
Huska, William, 54

Iams, Ross, 62
Imperial Japanese Navy: Battle of
    Coral Sea, 97–98; Battle of
    Midway and, 98–99; *Yamato*,
    111
Indian Wars, 33–40; Buffalo Soldiers
    in, 35–36
"In Flanders Fields" (MacCrae, J.),
    73
Iraq and Afghanistan Wars, 155–60
Irish, 17–18; in U.S. Army, 18; U.S.
    Army desertion of, 19–20

Jackson, Andrew, 9; Battle of New
    Orleans and, 11–14; Lafitte
    and, 11; Leveau and, 12; as
    president, 13; slavery and, 34;
    War of 1812 and, 9
Jackson, Thomas J. (Stonewall
    Jackson), 28, 64
Jamison, David F., 26
Japanese: American POWs and,
    80–81; Banzai attacks on,
    114, 118; Bataan Death March
    and, 78–79; *Hokka Maru*, 81;
    Makin Island raid and, 112–17;
    Mukden prison camp, 81–82;
    Shokaku (carrier), 98; South
    Pacific invasion by, 106–7;
    Yamato (battleship), 111. *See
    also* Imperial Japanese Navy
Johnson, Harris, 115

Johnson, Lyndon B., 136; Vietnam
    War and, 137, 141
Johnson, Percy, 129
Johnston, Albert Sidney, 28–29

Kennedy, John F., 136
Kettle Hill, Spanish American War,
    42–43
Key, Francis Scott, 10
Kissinger, Henry, 153
Kitty Hawk (carrier), 151
Korean War, 135; Bonham and,
    127–33; Womack and, 121–26
Kupperson, Sam, 125

Lafitte, Jean, 9–15; Battle of New
    Orleans and, 13; Jackson, A.,
    and, 11
Le Duc Tho. *See* Tho, Le Duc
Lee, Robert E., 18, 25; Battle of
    Bull Run and, 29; Grant and,
    30; Virginia's succession and,
    26–27
Leveau, Marie, 9–15; Battle of New
    Orleans and, 13; Jackson, A.,
    and, 12; voodoo and, 11–13
Lewis, Hugh, 100, 102
Lidice, Czechoslovakia, 111–12
Lincoln, Abraham, 26
Lincoln, Glenn, 110
Liverpool, England, 17–18
Long, John D., 42

MacArthur, Douglas, 55, 71, 78
MacCrae, George, 47, 49
Maddox (destroyer), 136
Madison, James, 10
Makin Island raid, 88–89, 112–17;
    retreat from, 115–17
Marine Corps: boot camp, 107–9;
    Butler in, 59–65; Roosevelt, J.,
    in, 86

Marine Raiders. *See* Carlson's Raiders
Marion, Francis, 1–8; British and search for, 5; early years of, 2–3; Gates and, 6; as leader, 4; raids, 6; as "Swamp Fox," 1, 5; Tarleton and, 4–5
Marion's Brigade, 4
Mays, Isaiah, 33–40; ambush, 37–38; as Buffalo Soldier, 33; enlistment, 35; final resting place of, 39–40; Medal of Honor received by, 38
McClellan, George, 29
McCrae, John, 73
McKinley, William, 41–43
McLean, Wilmer, 25–31
Meigs, Montgomery, 29
Mekong River, Vietnam, 152
Mexican Revolution, 51–52
Mexican War, 17–23; Battle of Buena Vista, 20; Battle of Convent Churubusco, 21; desertion during, 22; Irish American soldiers turned to Mexican patriots, 19; San Patricios and, 22–23
Miller, Jack, 90–91
The Missing in America Project, 39
Montalvo, Pete, 98
Mont Blanc (ship), 46–48
Morgan, Daniel, 7
Mukden prison camp, 81–82; liberation of, 83
Mussolini, Benito, 65

Nagasaki, Japan, 102
Native Americans, 34–35; Acoma, 75–76; BIA, 76; Cherokee War, 2–3; Indian Wars, 33–40
Nautilus (submarine), 112–13

Navy, U.S.: *Blue Jacket's Manual*, 95; boot camp, 94–95, 149–50; "Brown Water Navy," 152; glossary of terms, 103; polishing brass in, 86, 150; Skinner and, 93–103
Navy Inshore Operation Training Center (NIOTC), 152
Newberg, Pete, 99
The New Deal, 56, 67
New Hebrides Islands, 89–90
News coverage of Vietnam War, 137
Nimitz, Chester, 89
Nineteenth Amendment, 52–53
NIOTC. *See* Navy Inshore Operation Training Center
Nixon, Richard, 153
Nodland, Bud, 88–90, 110, 115
No Man's Land. *See* Christmas Truce in 1914
North Carolina, 122–23
Nuclear power, 102

Oakley, Annie, 56
Old Guard Riders, 39–40
O'Reilly, John. *See* Riley, John

Pardo, Bob, 141–47
Patman, Wright, 54
Patrol Boat River (PBR) squadron, 152
Patton, George S., 52; Angelo and, 55–56; Veterans' Bonus March and, 55
PBR squadron. *See* Patrol Boat River squadron
Pearl Harbor, 77, 87, 108–9, 112
Pershing, John J., 52; Butler and, 63
Peters, Michael, 136–37, 149–53; in charge of PBR squadron, 152; on Mekong River, 152; on USS *Harry E. Hubbard*, 150–51

Petigrew, James L., 26
Petross, Oscar, 114
Philadelphia, Pennsylvania, 65
Philippine American War, 60–61
Philippines: Bataan Peninsula, 78–79; WWII and, 78, 81
Plans, Operations and Medical Intelligence (POMI) office, 157
Plumbley, Merwyn, 114
Poison gas, use of, 72–73
Polishing brass, 150
POMI. *See* Plans, Operations and Medical Intelligence Office
Posttraumatic stress disorder (PTSD), 39
POW. *See* Prisoner-of-war
Prisoner-of-war (POW), 76; WWII, 79–82
Prohibition, 52–53, 65
PTSD. *See* Posttraumatic stress disorder

Reilly, John. *See* Riley, John
Remington, Fredric, 36
Revolutionary War: African Americans in, 36; Battle of Camden, 6; Battle of Cowpens, 7; Breed's Hill and, 1; British and, 4; Bunker Hill and, 1; Charleston's surrender in, 3; Marion and, 1–8; the South and, 3; South Carolina and, 2–3
Richardson, Richard, 5–6
Rickenbacker, Eddie, 70
Ricketts, Ernest, 97
Riley, John, 17–23; Battle of Buena Vista, 20; Battle of Convent Churubusco, 21; capture, trial, and conviction of, 21–22; desertion of U.S. Army, 19
Roosevelt, Franklin Delano, 71; Carlson's Raiders and, 87–88;

New Deal, 56, 67; plot to overthrow, 66–67; Roosevelt, J., and, 85–86
Roosevelt, James, 85–92; Carlson's Raiders and, 87–88; Makin Island raid, 88–89; in Marine Corps, 86; Roosevelt, F., and, 85–86
Roosevelt, Theodore: Medal of Honor received by, 43–44; Spanish American War and, 41–44
Rough Riders, 42–43

Sadler, Barry, 137
Sam, Vilbrun Guillaume, 61–62
San Juan Hill, Spanish American War, 42–43
San Patricios, 19–20; America's treatment of, 21–22; Battle of Convent Churubusco and, 21; capture, trial, and conviction of, 21–22; execution of, 21; Mexico's recognition of, 22–23. *See also* Mexican War
Santa Ana, Antonio López de, 20
September 11, 2001, terrorist attacks, 157
Shell shock, 39
Sheridan, Phil, 30
Shokaku (carrier), 98
Sigona, Suzanne, 46, 49
Skinner, Gordon, 93–103; Battle of Coral Sea and, 97–98; Battle of Midway and, 98–99; boot camp, 94–95; on *Sterlet*, 100–102; on USS *West Virginia*, 99–100; on USS *Yorktown*, 95–96
Slavery: Emancipation Proclamation and, 33–34; Jackson, A., and, 34

Solomon Islands, 91–92
South Carolina: Charleston's surren-
    der and, 3; Civil War and, 26;
    Revolutionary War and, 2–3
Southern United States: post–Civil
    War in, 34; in Revolutionary
    War, 3; in War of 1812, 10–11
South Pacific, Japanese invasion of,
    106–7
Spanish American War, 41–44; But-
    ler in, 60; Kettle Hill and San
    Juan Hill in, 42–43
SS *Lusitania*, 70
Sterlet (submarine), 100–102; war
    record of, 103
Stonewall Jackson. *See* Jackson,
    Thomas J.
Stratemeyer, George, 132
Submarine warfare, 45–46, 70; depth
    charge attacks and, 100–101;
    USS *Sterlet*, 100–102. *See also*
    specific submarines
Swamp Fox. *See* Marion, Francis
Sweeney, Thomas W., 21

Tarleton, Banastre: Marion and, 4–5;
    Richardson and, 5–6
"Tarleton's Quarter," 4
Task Force 17, 96–97
Thailand, Vietnam War and, 141
Tho, Le Duc, 153
Thomason, Clyde, 114
Ticonderoga (carrier), 151
Tonkin Gulf Resolution, 151
Truman, Harry S., 70–71, 124
Turner Joy (destroyer), 136
24th Infantry Regiment, 35

U-boats, 45–46
United States: Hispanics in, 156–57;
    western expansion of, 34; in
    WWI, 70. *See also* Southern

United States; Western United
    States
USS *Harry E. Hubbard*: in Gulf
    of Tonkin, 136–37, 150–51;
    in Vietnam War, 150–51; in
    WWII, 150
USS *Jupiter*, 96
USS *Lassen*, 96
USS *Maine*, 41, 60
USS *West Virginia*, 99–100
USS *Yorktown*, 95–96; Battle of
    Coral Sea and, 97–98; Battle
    of Midway and, 98–99; Task
    Force 17 and, 96–97

Valley Forge (carrier), 151
Veterans' Bonus March, 51–57; Pat-
    ton and, 55
Victoria, Queen, 69
Viet Cong, 152
Vietnam, 138–39; Binh Thuy, 153;
    Communism in, 136; Mekong
    River, 152
Vietnam War: antiwar protests,
    137; cease-fire agreement,
    153; country of Vietnam and,
    138–39; Goss and, 135–40;
    Gulf of Tonkin, 136, 151; John-
    son, L., and, 137, 141; news
    coverage of, 137; Pardo and,
    141–47; Peters and, 149–53;
    racial tensions in, 139; results
    of, 146–47; Thailand and, 141;
    USS *Harry E. Hubbard in*,
    150–51
Villa, Francisco "Pancho," 51–52
Virginia: Civil War and, 26–27; Ell-
    wood Plantation, 64
Vivar, Cecilia, 155–60; C-RAM
    operator training, 157–58;
    education of, 156–57; in Iraq,
    158–59

Wainwright, Jonathan, 79
War of 1812: Battle of New Orleans,
    9–14; cause of, 10; Lafitte and,
    9–15; Leveau and, 9–15; the
    South and, 10–11
War profiteering, 66
"War to End All Wars," 70. *See also*
    World War I
Washington, George, 6
Washington, William, 6
Western United States, 34; Buffalo
    Soldiers in, 36
Westmoreland, William, 137
Wilhelm II, Kaiser, 69
Womack, Bryant, 121–26; Medal of
    Honor awarded to, 126
Women in armed forces, 127
Women's Suffrage Movement, 53
Wood, Leonard, 42
Wooden, Faye, 13
World War I (WWI): Battle of Ypres,
    73; Butler in, 63–64; Canada
    in, 45; Christmas Truce in 1914,
    71–74; Halifax Disaster, 45–50;

historic figures from, 70–71;
    Hulse and, 69–74; United
    States in, 70; veterans, 54–57;
    Veterans' Bonus March, 51–57;
    as "War to End All Wars," 70
World War II (WWII): Antonio and,
    75–83; Bataan Death March,
    78–79; Battle of Midway
    and, 98–99, 111; Bauml and,
    105–19; Butaritari island,
    106–7; Carlson's Raiders and,
    85–92; Pearl Harbor, 77, 87,
    108–9, 112; Philippines and,
    78, 81; POWs in, 79–82; Roo-
    sevelt, J., 85–92; Skinner and,
    93–103; USS *Harry E. Hub-
    bard* in, 150
WWI. *See* World War I
WWII. *See* World War II

Yamato (battleship), 111
York, Alvin C., 70

Zouaves, 27–28

About the Author

PATRICK MENDOZA was an accomplished storyteller, author, and musician. He graduated from Metropolitan State University of Denver (formerly Metropolitan State College) with a degree in criminology. His published works include *Extraordinary People in Extraordinary Times: Heroes, Sheroes, and Villains* and *Four Great Rivers to Cross: Cheyenne History, Culture, and Traditions*, both with Libraries Unlimited, as well as *Between Midnight to Morning* and *Song of Sorrow: Massacre at Sand Creek*. Mendoza was a frequent contributing story author to the *Chicken Soup for the Soul* series of books.